ABOVE THE CLOUDS

ABOVE THE CLOUDS

KILIAN JORNET

How I Carved My Own Path
to the Top of the World

HarperOne
An Imprint of HarperCollins*Publishers*

HarperOne

Title-page photograph: Sébastien Montaz-Rosset

Mountain icon: pne | Adobe Stock

HarperCollins books may be purchased for educational, business, or sales promotional use. For information, please email the Special Markets Department at SPsales@harpercollins.com.

Originally published as *Res és impossible* in Spain in 2018 by Ara Llibres.

First HarperOne hardcover published 2020

FIRST EDITION

Translation by Charlotte Whittle

Designed by Janet Evans-Scanlon

Library of Congress Cataloging-in-Publication Data

Names: Jornet, Kilian, 1989– author.
Title: Above the clouds : how I carved my own path to the top of
    the world / Kilian Jornet ; translation by Charlotte Whittle.
Other titles: Res és impossible. English
Description: First edition. | San Francisco : HarperOne, 2020 | Originally
    published in Spain under the title: Res és impossible. | Translated from Spanish.
Identifiers: LCCN 2020008219 (print) | LCCN 2020008220 (ebook) | ISBN
    9780062965035 (hardcover) | ISBN 9780062965042 (trade paperback) | ISBN
    9780062965059 (ebook)
Subjects: LCSH: Jornet, Kilian, 1989– | Mountaineers–Spain–Biography. |
    Athletes–Spain–Biography.
Classification: LCC GV199.92.J67 A313 2020 (print) | LCC GV199.92.J67
    (ebook) | DDC 796.522092 [B]–dc23
LC record available at https://lccn.loc.gov/2020008219
LC ebook record available at https://lccn.loc.gov/2020008220

20 21 22 23 24   LSC   10 9 8 7 6 5 4 3 2 1

Contents

ABOVE THE CLOUDS

Introduction

I t's not like I woke up one morning with some transcendental resolution to start running.

I've been running mountains since the very beginning of my life, and since then I have spent my days counting the blueness of the lakes, the sharpness of the ridges, the length of the sunsets, and, well, some boring stuff like meters climbed and the miles behind and in front of me.

I wasn't like most kids growing up. The posters in my childhood bedroom were of Matterhorn, the Toblerone mountain in Switzerland, and a panorama called the Roof of the World, showing the range of Everest and the surrounding mountains. Eventually I climbed Matterhorn, and sometime after that I climbed Everest. When I ran up and down Matterhorn, it was to break a record, but Everest was different. I approached Everest with the idea to try a new way of mountain climbing. Four years separated my climb of Matterhorn and Everest, but mostly what separated them was my realization that I was living a life of contradictions. I ran fast to live a slow lifestyle. I needed solitude to be myself and social interactions to make a living. I loved the adrenaline of a race and the calm of the world above 8,000 meters. I enjoyed discovering remote mountains, but to protect them, I now realize it might have been better if I hadn't visited them at all. I *am* those contradictions, and how I deal with them is also who I am. There will always be consequences to my actions, positive or negative, and those consequences might affect only myself or affect a large amount of people.

As a teenager, I learned how to race in the mountains. It is all about training, getting in shape, executing the perfect movements, but beyond the physical, it is about how a runner or climber *sees* the mountains. Are they merely a playground to race on? Are they a stadium on which to perform your sport? Or are they something else entirely?

When I climbed Matterhorn, I viewed mountains as my playground, the source of my greatest joy and fun and pleasure, and as my stadium, where I competed. Then, after some encounters with a few special humans you'll read about in these pages, the fury of the mountains emerged in my life, and my stadium started to fall apart. Competition in sports is about performance. The time on the clock. When you cross the finish line. When your competitors do the same. In federated sports, this performance is judged by rules and regulations. But in the mountains, these rules and regulations are meaningless. Mountains are (still) a space of freedom, where lawlessness reigns for the good of everyone.

DIDIER DELSALLE HAS BEEN ON TOP OF EVEREST. ON MAY 14, 2005, HE landed with his helicopter on the 8,848-meter summit. If he told you that he reached the summit of Everest, he wouldn't be lying, although most of us in the mountain-climbing world would disagree. But where is the line we can draw between achieving the greatest feat—reaching the summit—and climbing the distance to get there? How many steps are considered effort *enough* to claim an ascent? What I've learned is that every shortcut is a personal decision you must live with, and every achievement is the same.

When it comes to climbing mountains, the *reaching* should never compromise the journey to get there. That's why when I climbed Everest, I did it alone with no assistance—not to simply step on the summit but to see what I was able to endure in my journey getting there. Four years before, when I ran up and down Matterhorn faster than anyone before, I was obsessed only with the achievement, researching the past, emulating how the fastest person before me had done it, and using his rules, as it was a competition. I was racing him. On Everest, I raced myself.

When I started traveling far to do a run or a race or a climb, I considered it just a part of the job. But today I'm questioning how much of that travel is making a negative impact on the natural world I love so much. Does the answer "Because that's just how it is" make it okay? In the long run, climbing Everest has likely been a very selfish and absurd activity, but what I understand from writing this book is that the path I have taken to climb it and the encounters I have had on that road have changed the way I see not only the mountain but also myself, and the connection between humans and nature has made me, I hope, a more committed human with those contradictions. Throughout these pages I try to explain this journey.

In the end, *Above the Clouds* is not about what I have achieved but about what I have experienced, about feeling at peace with my values when I do something and embracing the possibility of change and failure as a reward for my soul.

The Farewell

My lips said *"I love you"* when what they really wanted to admit was *"I'm sorry."*

I kept forcing the words out, trying to make excuses: "Don't worry," "I'll be careful" . . . but I knew no excuse would seem reasonable to her for setting out on an adventure that could lead to my death on the world's highest mountain. Yet I need to climb mountains to feel alive, even if I risk death.

I managed to mumble, "Goodbye," with an uneasy feeling that I was being selfish and narcissistic. I definitely am those things. I took my backpack out of the trunk, accidentally slamming the lid shut. Dazed by the sudden loud noise, and this strange silence between us, I finally tapped on the back windshield to let her know she could leave.

IT WAS EARLY AUGUST, BUT THE AIR WAS BRISK. THE SCENT OF THE sea filled my lungs. Tromsø is a fishing port on a little island surrounded by fjords and mountains, above the Arctic Circle in northern Norway. For a few weeks in summer, the sun doesn't set; it's always daytime. It's as if time means nothing: grandparents go out for a midnight stroll, and you can see your neighbors fixing their balconies or tiling their roofs in the wee hours of the morning. A collective drunkenness seems to take hold of the region for a single, never-ending day. But the sun is gentle and never rises high in the sky, doing circles above the horizon, painting it with a thick layer of pastel colors, yellow and orange tones, sometimes flooded with intense red.

The airport, where I said goodbye to the woman I love, lies at one end of the island. As Emelie drove away, I blew her a silent kiss. I didn't want to look back, so I walked into the airport, trying to let my eyes dry before I went up to the check-in desk. I was setting out on a journey that would take me to the summit of Everest, aware of the difficulties and dangers that lay ahead. Despite everything, at no point did I reconsider this decision.

A FEW HOURS EARLIER, EMELIE AND I HAD GONE FOR A RUN TOGETHER. Taking advantage of the continual light, we went out at night, after dinner, to stretch our legs and clear our minds after a tense and stressful few days of organizing a race for a few hundred runners. In the last few days, the phone calls, car rides back and forth, and hand squeezes had been near constant. Running together, just the two of us, would be a much-needed cleansing exercise.

We set off along a narrow path, leaving the noise of the city behind. We wanted the mountains to shelter us. The wind's soft murmur replaced the radio programs floating out of the houses and shops in town, and a pure, fresh breeze replaced the stifling air among the crowds and the smoke. Gradually, our legs began to feel lighter and lose the stiffness of the last few days. We climbed to the top of the first peak and ran on without stopping. We left the dirt path for the fields, climbing a new route. The frosty grass soaking our feet contrasted with the hard, dry surface of the black asphalt. Little by little, our hearts began to beat at a shared rhythm, echoing the thump of our steps.

We ran side by side, steeped in a feeling of peace and serenity that contrasted with the whirlwind of the previous days. But happiness can't continue forever; this calm was the prelude to our farewell. Though from time to time we opened our mouths to try to say what needed to be said between us, sound didn't emerge.

Later, when we drove to the airport, neither of us could express what we'd both been feeling for a long time: fear and regret. And leaving it unsaid, we made a pact of silence that would last until I returned from the expedition.

THROUGH THE AIRPLANE WINDOW, THE CITY SHRANK UNTIL IT DISAP-peared. I stared through the glass at the plane's shadow as we flew over fjords and still-snowy peaks, mountains and valleys. I knew many of those paths and crests, but I saw new paths from the air and imagined myself running along them on my return. At that moment, though, I was leaving them behind, too, and I hoped they would forgive me for going in search of another.

I thought of the things I should have told Emelie while we were running together, to relieve the suffering she was sure to experience while we were far apart. A subtle joke or a clever comment, but I'm no good at thinking of quick things to say on the spot. I feel at peace in the mountains because, as Italian mountaineer Reinhold Messner said, they are not fair or unfair; they are just dangerous. And, in danger, you can apply a certain logic when it comes to making what you think will be the right decision. In the mountains, I never waver, but in the more jagged terrain of relationships, I am paralyzed.

THE EARTH DISAPPEARED AS WE ENTERED A CLOUD, AND THE TURBU-lence made me snap back into the present. Leaving always brings a wave of contradictory feelings: the fleeting freedom of escape mixed with nostalgia for the warmth and familiarity I've left behind.

In the plane's hold was a suitcase weighing exactly fifty pounds. I had scrupulously calculated how to pack for this trip, with all the equipment I would need to conquer a high peak. There was no room for anything else, not even a pen.

The preparations had gone almost perfectly, or at least that's how it seemed to me. I had spent the last month in the Alps, most of the time above 4,000 meters, preparing my lungs and body for Everest's impossibly high summit. I felt comfortable at a high altitude and was ready for the technical difficulties of the mountain.

Before an assault on a summit, there is a moment that is impossible to quantify. It goes beyond the miles you've covered and the inevitable circumstances you've overcome. This is when you realize you have the necessary calm for the ascent. The sense of safety that takes hold when you feel comfortable in a terrain where, if you had more sense, you ought not to feel so safe. I had noticed I was in that exact state of mind as I finished my training in the Alps, and I still felt this way on the plane ride to Everest, where my risk threshold would be higher than usual. On the one hand, this was comforting, but on the other, it filled me with a fear of myself, since I didn't know for sure what I would do if faced with a choice between my desire to climb the mountain and my sense of self-preservation, which keeps me calm and protects me from crossing boundaries with no return.

The flight attendant pushed the dinner cart to the row where I was seated. She smiled and asked me to choose between the chicken and rice and the vegetable pasta. I decided on the pasta. Like clones of one another, all the passengers on the flight began the same dance at once: we opened the tiny cardboard package, removed the foil protecting the food, burned our fingers to confirm that it was too hot, then tore open the transparent cutlery wrapper and took out a fork to spear the four lettuce leaves. We inspected the pudding on the left of the tray with a sidelong glance. *Is it chocolate?*

Without knowing very well how, I had ended up with a tub of processed macaroni and was now stirring it around with a disposable fork. I decided I was full. I placed everything in a pile as best I could, left it on the corner of the table, and waited for the flight attendant to come back and take it away.

Intercontinental flights are like a long trip to a mall in a large city. There are always children crying and teenagers whispering, letting out the occasional scream or guffaw. Bad food, shiny offers for products you'll never use, and movies, music, or games—it doesn't matter which—to pass the time.

I tried to escape the productivity traps these kinds of environments set by opening the notebook in which I was planning to journal my expedition and write down important things like daily activities, measurements of the slopes and the altitude, a record of how I felt while acclimating, meteorological data. And I gave it a try, but amid all the people crammed together in such a claustrophobic setting, I couldn't make a single mark on the blank page.

Angry with myself, I gave in to temptation and searched for a movie on the little screen on the seat back in front of me. Luckily, I fell asleep soon after the opening credits.

In the dream, I entered a forest. The trees were large but weren't the enormous sequoias you see in the United States. They belonged to a traditional forest, like in the Pyrenees, but were disproportionately large. It was like seeing everything from the height of a child or a small animal.

Despite my calm, I was scared. Deep in the forest, everything moved at a dizzying speed. I began to walk. I wanted to get out, but everything was spinning around me, preventing me from finding or choosing the right path. I began to run, but the forest kept spinning and moving just as fast. My legs wouldn't obey me and felt like they were made of lead; they were frozen to the mossy ground carpeted with pine needles. When I finally seemed able to free myself, the forest lurched like a boat in the midst of a storm and I fell.

I could make out the shadows of animals passing between the trees. There seemed to be dozens. They were giant and began to surround me, the circle in which I was trapped closing in around me. When the animals were finally so close that they seemed about to crush me, I realized that in fact it was only one animal, a kind of long-legged mammoth running with enormous strides. But when I looked closer, I realized the beast that had cornered me wasn't a mammoth but an enormous rabbit or hare.

Suddenly, I heard a knock on a tree as if someone was

chopping it down with an axe. Chop, chop. The sound was right next to me. And I felt the hare, or whatever it was, grab me by the shoulder. Chop, chop.

"Excuse me, would you like something to drink?" the flight attendant asked, waking me up with a start.

I let her know with a sleepy gesture that I didn't want anything, and she pushed the cart loaded with drinks to the row behind me. That's when it dawned on me: It was Petita! A hare I had found as a child, on a stormy day, in the forest behind the mountain refuge where we lived. In my dream she was huge, but when I rescued her she was an injured baby. That afternoon, all those years ago, I took her home, gave her some food and water, and laid her in my bedroom to sleep with me. But after a few days, she had recovered and filled the room with droppings, and wouldn't stop moving under the sheets while I slept, and my parents asked me to let her go. I didn't want to. She was mine! I had found her and rescued her, had built her a big pen outside the refuge for her to run around in, and fed her each afternoon when I got home from school.

But one day after a few months of keeping her, when I went to see her after class, I found that Petita had died. I cried and cried, asking myself over and over what I'd done wrong. I didn't realize that I had killed her by trying to take care of her. She had chosen to die rather than remain alive and imprisoned. Some animals are meant to live free.

THREE DAYS AFTER GETTING OFF THE PLANE, I FELT FAR AWAY FROM all that I'd left behind: the frosty fields that had soaked my feet as I ran with Emelie in the silence we both had wanted to break without knowing how. *Why didn't we say anything to each other?* Her hugs were far away now. So were the city, the traffic, the noise, and my worry that the car in front of us would make me late to the airport. So were my notebook full of preparation notes and Petita, the hare in my dream.

Now I was here on Everest in the springtime, attempting to ascend and descend the mountain in the fastest time, and I was in a fine mess.

If I looked ahead, behind, or above, I saw only white enveloping everything. And below, my legs pierced the snow. And the silence was so intense and absolute that I could hear a distant, piercing whistle in my ears.

In fact, there was no silence: I breathed deeply; the wind blew in violent gusts; snowflakes fell from the sky, rebelling against the air, flurrying at me from every direction, driving against my coat, which made a rhythmic flapping sound. There was so much noise that it ended up canceling itself out. It was not silent, but I felt silence. In my eyes, my ears . . . a single shade of white that traced a diagonal path up ahead allowed me to see the steep slope I was tackling. But a few feet ahead, the slope disappeared in the midst of the storm. Behind me, the deep path I'd cut had vanished almost immediately beneath the snow. *Let's go, Kilian. One more step.* The snow came up to my knees and would soon be compacted by the wind.

I could intuit with all my senses that in a few seconds this 2,000-meter wall, which had seemed inoffensive just two hours ago, was going to turn into an enormous unsteady sheet, a trap hiding an avalanche. I drove my ice axes in as deeply as I could. I'd lost track of my fellow climbers, who were somewhere behind me. I couldn't see them. The thick fog had swallowed them.

I took another step on this fifty-degree slope on the north-east face of Everest, hoping the snowfall that had accumulated in the last few hours wouldn't detach from the wall and sweep down the mountainside. And hoping it wouldn't pull me down with it.

Before I attempted each step, I thought: *Is this the last mountain I'll climb? How the hell did I get this far?*

IT'S A LONG STORY. IT DIDN'T BEGIN WHEN I FIRST STARTED TRAINING to climb Everest in the summer. Or when I went back in the fall and the winter of that year to train again. It didn't begin when I said goodbye to Emelie in the spring of the following year, headed to Everest to finally attempt my goal. Or when I took the plane to Nepal, or even when I dreamed of exploring Everest when I was young. Though I might not have been aware of it, this story began long before, 6,000 feet above sea level in Spain. My home.

Training

There are people who train to compete, and there are those who compete to train.

I belong to the second group. The goal of competing can provide a source of motivation, but it isn't necessary for the training—far from it.

I STILL REMEMBER THE FIRST TIME I FOUND EXTREME AND ALMOST perverse enjoyment in the leg pain and breathlessness I felt as I ascended a steep slope and gave it my all. It happened one late spring day in my early teens, as I cycled around the French department of Ariège in Occitanie, with Joan, the father of a friend from school. The sky was blue, and the heat was suffocating. We were climbing one of the many mountain passes in the region; I can't remember which one. We took a narrow road through abandoned villages and fields without livestock, and Joan yelled back advice to me as he pedaled ahead.

"You have to stop doing miles just for the sake of it, and climbing mountains with no rhyme or reason. You have to treat it like a job. Imagine you're building up credit," he said, "to use the day you really want to go *fast*."

I pretended to listen to him, but all that really interested me was covering more miles each day than the day before, and going faster and faster. When the conversation dragged on too long and I didn't want to keep listening, I sped up to provoke an attack so I would have an excuse to give it my all and end up exhausted. My legs hurt, we were going faster and faster, and I began to feel short of breath and a strange kind of pleasure, until I saw a sign that said we were only half a mile away from the highest point of the pass. I noticed a surprising sadness inside me.

"Come on, the best part is coming up," Joan encouraged me, thinking of the descent.

"Yeah," I answered, "but I think I'd like the climb to go on forever."

I WAS TWELVE YEARS OLD, AND THAT SUMMER I WANTED TO COMPETE in the Three Nations Cycling Tour, which went from Puigcerdà to Andorra and passed through France, then back to the capital of La Cerdanya, covering a total of over 150 kilometers. I thought I should get ready to compete, not just sustain myself by cycling for hours and hours, so I started writing down in a notebook all the training and rides I was doing. Though I had been walking long distances and cycling alone or with my parents for years, for the first time I was consciously training for a concrete goal.

That summer, I participated in the Three Nations. In the fall, I did the 80-kilometer Caballos del Viento route, and I also entered the Centro de Tecnificación de Esquí de Montaña, the national youth team for mountain skiing, since my mother thought I should channel my energy in an orderly way. It was lucky that I enrolled, because that's where I met two of the most influential people in my life: Jordi Canals, the center's director, and Maite Hernández, my first trainer.

IN THE SUMMER OF 2004, MAITE HERNÁNDEZ GAVE ALL OF HER YOUNG students a gift: a little stone. That spring, she had climbed the north face of Everest as part of a women's expedition and had brought that little keepsake down from the mountain for us. I stowed mine away like the treasure it was.

Jordi had already been to Everest twice, as part of the first Catalan expeditions in 1983 and 1985, when Òscar Cadiach, Toni Sors, and Carles Vallès reached the summit. Jordi telling us about his experiences taught us to perform as well as we could in competitions, but also to be safe and fully equipped on a mountain. I have the impression he, in fact, doubted that any of his students would end up becoming professionals and contend for world championships, and that's why he focused on making sure we first enjoyed the mountains and the effort.

During one of those trainings, as we were climbing the Tossa d'Alp for the second or third time that day, a few feet before reaching the highest slopes, those of us who were up ahead, making a huge effort to catch up with Jordi—who was climbing calmly—stopped to take off our skins to go down and do another ascent. He planted himself ahead of us with a hand on his chin, striking a thoughtful pose, and, in a sarcastic tone so as not to sound too important, he let slip:

"The summit's up there, you know!"

We looked at him to see if he was being serious. We had come there to train, to cover the meters of that slope without *wasting* any time. Even if it would take us only twenty seconds to reach the highest point—taking off our skis, walking a little to the summit, then putting them back on—it would cause us to lose a couple of minutes on each ascent and disrupt the pace we had set.

Jordi was adamant. "Well, do we ski and climb mountains, or not? And mountain climbing is all about reaching the summit, right?"

THERE IS NO EQUALITY IN COMPETITIVE SPORTS. IF, FOR EXAMPLE, I had wanted to be a basketball player, even if I had been passionately committed, tried with all my might, and broken my back with the effort, the truth is, I wouldn't have gotten very far. Already, as a young kid in the admission tests for the Centro de Tecnificación, I showed the necessary qualities to forge a future in mountain endurance sports. Despite being at the lower end of the group for strength and explosive power, I felt comfortable when we ran uphill, and I could hold my own alongside those who were older than me. It must have been because I had a high capacity for recovery and a small, light body, which helped me a lot in the beginning. We can't choose our genes or our build, and they'll be with us for our whole lives. But they're far from enough in determining who will be successful. Natural predisposition should always be accompanied by hard work and passion. I've had the good luck to be able to bring these requirements together—something not all athletes can do. There are those who approach their activity passionately. Maybe their body and their abilities don't match their passion, and after years of stoical persistence they can achieve great results, but without the necessary extra factors, they can't achieve full excellence. There are also people with immense ability but who don't love their sport enough to have a successful career. They don't put enough effort into it and end up unmotivated.

Though it might be hard to believe, I didn't plan to practice mountain sports. It was my parents who introduced me to this world, when I was very little, as they also did with my sister. We lived in a mountain refuge at an altitude of 2,000 meters, and the shelves were filled with books by mountaineers Kurt Diemberger, Roger Frison-Roche, and Walter Bonatti. During school vacations, we always went somewhere in the Pyrenees or the Alps to *do* mountains.

It may seem like a paradox, but often such an intense immersion in an activity can lead a child, in adolescence, to do exactly the opposite of what their parents want. But I imagine both my sister and I still love the mountains because we built a much deeper relationship with them that went beyond the simple pleasure of practicing a sport.

I remember that when we were still little kids clinging to our mother's legs, sometimes, after dinner, after we'd put on our pajamas and brushed our teeth, our mother would take us by the hand and lead us outside. We would go into the dark forest with no light to guide us. We would stray from the paths and walk on the moss and fallen branches until we could no longer see the light from the house, and then she would let go of our hands, tell us to listen to the sounds of the forest, and find our way back to the refuge alone. At first, we were afraid of the sounds and the darkness. "What if there's a wolf? What if we get lost and can't find our way back?" and then we would get frightened and run for our mother's protection. But gradually we grew accustomed to the darkness and the night's murmurs: a branch creaking because of the drop in temperature at night, the hum of the air stirred by a partridge flapping its wings as it took off, or the whistle of the wind through the trees. When we heard all this, we regained our calmness, greeted the wind and the animals, and followed the signs leading us back to the refuge. In this natural and almost unconscious way, we learned from our mother to *be part* of the mountain.

YEARS WENT BY, AND WHEN I WAS A TEENAGER, I DISCOVERED THAT I had masochistic tendencies. That was when I put the last, indispensable piece of the puzzle in place, completing the picture that would open the door to being a professional athlete. I had put the first piece in place the day I began to sculpt my muscles and tendons and to move naturally over uneven terrain, during trips into the mountains with my parents. The long hours on mountain trails had also trained my heart for stamina. Now my body was primed.

Despite being a good student, I was bored by the scene at school. I had zero social life and didn't even try to make friends. I was interested only in learning. While my classmates waited impatiently for the bell to ring so they could go have a drink, play in the park, race home to play video games, or try to hook up with someone, all I could think about was putting on my sneakers to go for a run. I wanted to feel exhaustion in my heart and pain in my legs again.

I took advantage of any free moment to train. Before sunrise, if I could, I slipped out to ski with my mom, or just went out for a run, or slid the 25 kilometers from home to school on my roller skis. At lunchtime, instead of heading to the dining hall, I went out to bounce around on the outskirts of town, and on the three days when Maite Hernández had me do strength training, I went to the city's gym. When I came home in the afternoon, I'd barely even put my backpack in my room before taking off on my bike or going for a run. If Maite told me to rest, I was glued to the TV, watching the DVD *La Tecnica dei Campioni* over and over again, in which the movements of the greatest ski mountaineers, such as Stéphane Brosse, Rico Elmer, Florent Perrier, and Guido Giacomelli, were analyzed in simple terms. I didn't care if I had no friends or people called me weird because all I wanted to know was how far my body could go.

This dynamic continued in college. Apart from my classmates who were also involved in sports, my social life was limited to the people I saw at races. I never went on any end-of-semester trips, never put in an appearance at parties or dances, and never touched a drop of alcohol, except at times when I was, shall we say, forced. I avoided these kinds of situations because I had the impression that they were just a waste of time and energy, and that it would be more helpful for me to train or rest.

If you're thinking right now that when I was young I tended to disconnect from my surroundings and had a closed outlook, you're probably not far off. I had no doubt, from the moment I decided to dedicate my life to sports, that for some doors to open for me, others would have to close forever.

To me, sport doesn't mean a life full of sacrifices but rather one full of choices. You make choices about where you want to go, and the secret lies in prioritizing what you really want to do and sticking to the plan you've made without hesitation. At the end of the day, what's more important? Having friends and a girlfriend or striving to become the world champion of your discipline?

I BEGAN TO TRAIN MYSELF DURING MY EARLY YEARS IN COLLEGE. FOR five years, with Maite as my coach, I learned the basic rules of training, like rationing my efforts and understanding the relationship between workload, rest, and overcompensation, and planning my training in the mid- to long-term according to my goals. In those five years, I managed to turn the masochist, thoughtlessly tackling ascents, into someone who could train to win important races. In addition to Maite's patience as I incorporated these ideas and put them into practice, the other factor that helped me improve was an injury when I was eighteen, which kept me out of action for six months. The surgeon who operated on me noted that I might not be able to perform as well as before. The anxiety he instilled in me and the realization that an accident can ruin a career inspired me to study the factors that influence athletic performance as if I were possessed: biomechanics, training, psychology, technique, equipment, diet . . . It was a good lesson. Having to deal with a defective leg was not a hindrance but rather allowed me to open my mind to important decisions I would need to make on my journey. The questions I asked myself about the workings of the mind and body intensified in the years when I studied physical education in college. But I have always been impatient. I was incapable of waiting around to *learn* about conclusions that might be of use to me. Now that I was winning races and felt confident in my daily training, I began to experiment with my body.

My idea was to push a specific aspect of my body to the limit, such as my metabolism's ability to work at aerobic capacity with no energy input, or the possibility to repeat anaerobic exercises at a high altitude and then recover, to mention a couple of things that preoccupied me. If I solved these mysteries, not only could I take advantage of the results and theoretical adaptations, but also I would feel the potential and the limits of my body, in all its rigor, with total precision.

Of course, to conduct those experiments I had to take advantage of periods when I wasn't competing, so I had enough time to recover if things got out of control. I also had to conduct them on safe, familiar terrain that was nearby, in case I got hurt and had to rush home.

DURING MY COLLEGE YEARS, I WENT TO ONLY ONE PARTY, WHICH A classmate tricked me into attending, after one of these training experiments. And even today, I still believe I let myself be convinced because my will was crushed by exhaustion.

It must have been the spring of 2008. I was in Font-Romeu and wanted to test my body's capacity for action without any energy input. In other words, I wanted to know how many days I could spend training and running without eating anything. To find out, I went about my life as usual, running two to four hours in the morning and another hour in the afternoon, but eliminated all meals. I had to adjust the logistics ahead of time since I had no doubt that if there was food in the room, my hunger would take over. I emptied the fridge and the pantry, handed the contents to a friend, and gave him strict instructions not to feed me anything, even if I showed up begging in the wee hours. I only allowed myself to drink as much water as I liked.

I should clarify that all I wanted to find out through this experiment was how long I could run without added energy, with only the fat and muscle protein my body already had as fuel, and to study the stages of the process. I never for a moment thought of it as a weight-loss therapy or a way to discover if I could perform as well while eating less.

Unfortunately, in extreme sports, especially in disciplines in which weight is very important—and that includes ski mountaineering—many athletes are obsessed with losing weight, and for them, this is a recurring and highly relevant problem. I know athletes who have spent half a lifetime going hungry to maintain their target weight; others who get up at the crack of dawn to ransack the fridge because they can't stand to train anymore without eating; and those who induce vomiting after they eat, to trick their hunger and keep their weight down.

If we have to accept that extreme sports are unhealthy because we take our bodies to the limit and run the risk of injury, we should also be clear that we must be the ones to manage our own bodies and that they should always be under our control. When we're guided by our basic urges, we've already lost. If we're not in control of what we do, the sport loses its beauty and leads us into a downward spiral that can plunge us into the darkness of depression or illnesses like bulimia and anorexia. In extreme cases, we lose our sense of the meaning of life and throw it away. Sadly, this continues to be a taboo topic in the sports world, but it needs to be brought out into the open.

Let's get back to the experiment in Font-Romeu.

After removing all the food from my room and with the will to reach the end, I began to run. Since I was young, my body has been used to running for hours with my parents without eating anything, so the first day, I didn't notice any decline in my performance. Well, to be honest, at the end of the day, when I was alone in my room, I was ravenous. After a night of hunger, in the morning I set off on my usual route, which took between three and four hours. I went out to the Font-Romeu Hermitage and up to the highest part of the ski slopes, down the other side, and looped around one of the lakes, climbing one of the peaks of the Bouillouses or Pic Carlit. On my way back, I headed toward the area above the ski slopes and then back down to the apartments. During the gentle ascent to the slopes, I could assess the effects of my experiment clearly.

My overall pace had hardly changed, since I was able to run at a moderate speed for hours with no great difficulty, but whereas I usually sped up as fast as I could during that climb to the slopes, after a second day without eating, it was impossible. No matter how hard I tried, I couldn't sprint. My body had become a tractor running on diesel that could move slowly across great distances but had lost its power.

On the third and fourth days, everything stayed more or less the same. But on the fifth, during my morning run, I fainted and collapsed on the ground.

Luckily, I came round by myself a short time later. I hadn't been in any danger because the path was well traveled, and if necessary, someone would have been able to help. I went back to the hermitage, went to my friend's room, and ate.

That same week, I was persuaded to go to an end-of-semester party. I spent a moment or two in the limelight, because I passed out drinking an orange juice.

SINCE THEN, I HAVE PRACTICED A METHOD FOR GETTING TO KNOW MY body and the benefits of better training. I have experimented with sleep, hydration, and several kinds of training, running at high altitudes, trying out different equipment, and practicing a hundred hours a week. Most of these experiments have ended up in disaster. I didn't perform the way I hoped to, and I was so tired that I didn't get much out of it. Despite this, through each of these experiments, I found clues and ideas for improving and pushing my limits.

My most recent experiment allowed me to explore how I adjust to high altitudes. When I began the Summits of My Life project in 2012, during which I sought to set ascent and descent records on the world's highest peaks, this was one of my greatest concerns. And ever since my first trip to the Himalayas, in 2013, each year I have done at least one expedition or spent a period at high altitude trying out different methods of acclimation— always with the intention of not staying long, because there are more interesting things in life than spending three months at the foot of a mountain.

Though I acclimated well on my first trip to the Himalayas, I would have liked to be able to climb faster. Then, in 2014, I went to Denali, Alaska, and I burned out. Despite feeling good at the end of the first few days—we were there two weeks—

after going up and down the mountain quickly, I had no energy left. Later that same year, I went to Aconcagua. I wanted to do an acclimation exercise in the Alps, and it worked out well. After four days in Argentina, I reached the summit of Aconcagua, but later, my desire to train faster and faster had a negative effect, and the day I broke a record, I suffered a cerebral edema, completely losing control of my legs in the first half of the descent. They seemed to be made of Jell-O; I lost my balance and kept falling onto the ground.

Over the next three years, I went to the Himalayas and tried out various strategies: low activity, high activity, gradual or rapid training . . . In the end, when it came to the expedition to Everest, my acclimation and high-altitude performance were perfect.

I KNOW THE WAY I TRAIN CAN BE DANGEROUS. FOR ONE REASON: MY method is oriented toward figuring out my limits. In the worst-case scenario, and depending on what I'm trying to accomplish, I could end up overstepping those limits and risking my life. It's different from preparing your body to be at its peak and in the best possible condition on a given day to take on a challenge or break a record. Very different.

Had I kept running without eating after having passed out, during that experiment in Font-Romeu—which I don't recommend anyone try—I have no idea what the consequences might have been. If, on another occasion, I hadn't hydrated after aching all over and noticing that my urine was blacker than coal, I would have suffered acute kidney damage. These are extreme cases—there's no doubt about it.

The purpose of my experiments wasn't just physical; they also allowed me to gain confidence in myself. I knew firsthand what I was capable of, and I learned to suffer and get the most out of my body, squeezing every last drop of energy from it when I lost my strength or my motivation dwindled. You have to be fast to win races, but that alone isn't enough to make you competitive. You must be aware that you can't overcome your body's physiological limits. On the other hand, if you want to do as well as possible, what you *can* do is build up an armor made of different pieces: mental preparation, technique, the kind of equipment you use, and your strategy. Your body possesses immense knowledge and, when necessary, sends signals asking you if you want to keep going or not. Those warning bells are called *fainting*, *leg pain*, *hallucinations*, and *vomiting*. Whether you want to break the final barrier depends on you and you alone.

There is one more limit, a psychological one. This one is called *fear*. It's a great travel companion and has two sides. On the one hand, if you ignore it, you can overcome all your psychological obstacles and gain a true understanding of how far you can go. On the other, if you don't learn how to listen to it, it can end up leading you into an abyss. You must assess which is the better partner to dance with.

I LOVE PHYSICAL TRAINING. YEARS AND YEARS OF WORK AND ALMOST total abstinence in search of the ideal, fleeting moment that ends in a sigh. It's different from intellectual activity, in which the knowledge you constantly acquire and accumulate stays with you. When you work with the body, nothing you win ever belongs to you or lasts forever, since you always have to keep training just as hard, to keep the bar as high as you want it to be.

Many athletes train from childhood to compete and be champions, but only a very few chosen ones end up making it. Often the result is people with hugely inflated egos, carrying around a backpack full of frustration. I believe that children should be coached not to win but to train. If this were the general pattern, everyone would have their slice of delicious cake, and the competition would just be the cherry on top. I was lucky enough that this was the first thing Maite Hernández and Jordi Canals taught me. Training was necessary, competition was optional, and the time to compete would come when it came. This approach turned out to be very useful to me years later, when I was climbing Mount Everest.

Maite and Jordi also taught me to be methodical and analytical, to note everything about my performance so I could analyze it later and identify anything that hadn't worked out well. This meant tallying everything up: the time and kilometers I trained, the number of hours I slept—and whether I had taken advantage of them—and more.

I wrote everything down, without missing a detail, in a notebook with square, ruled pages—I was meticulous. Every two weeks, Maite and I would get together to review it and talk about what I should do in the next two weeks. From her, I learned the importance of taking precise notes and not leaving out any detail that might be important later.

I REMEMBER ONE DAY WHEN I WAS TRAINING AT THE CENTER. IT WAS very hot, and as usual I had no liquid with me. After a few hours of activity, I was dying of thirst, and Maite offered me some water. When I leapt forward to grab her flask, she suddenly snatched it away.

"Haven't you learned anything from what I've taught you? Imagine if I had a cold and you drank this water that I've been drinking, with all its viruses and bacteria. What about the week of training we have planned?"

When I began to train alone, I continued with the methodical task of writing everything down. In 2006, I made an Excel document where I recorded everything: each activity, every day I was sick, every car or plane journey that affected my rest, every public event that made me lose concentration when training, every strange or pleasant sensation.

Interpreting all this data is a complex task that requires me to keep my feet on the ground. I have to be as honest as I can in my notes. If I'm not, a few years from now, when I want to know why I did so well in a given week, everything I might extrapolate from these records would be wrong. Despite the fact that I'm the only person who reads this document, sometimes it's hard to avoid falling into the trap of false modesty or overvaluation.

For example, one day I wrote:

"February 16, 2005. Pulse 42 when I woke up, 2 hours 30 minutes of ski mountaineering—2,300 meters. 30-minute warm-up, 6 sets of 15 seconds at maximum, and 5 sets of 6 minutes at 180 pulse with 1 minute rest. In the first rest periods I went down well to 130 pulse, from the third on I didn't go below 150. Afternoon stretches. I have a cold."

And another day:

"June 14, 2011. Morning: Les Houches, Mont Blanc (4 hours

7 minutes), a bit tired, but I can still force myself. 4,200-meter slope. Afternoon: gentle bike 1 hour 30 minutes, 300 meters, legs heavy but in good cardio shape. Interview and trip."

The notes were still important as far as races and goals were concerned, because I could see from them whether what I'd done had been of any use:

"August 14, 2013. Sierre-Zinal, 20 miles, 2h 34m 15s: legs very heavy from the beginning, I feel good cardio-wise, but zero legs, pain in left hamstring and right calf. I can't take the pace, not fast enough on flat ground."

"August 30, 2008. UTMB [Ultra-Trail du Mont Blanc], 100 miles—32,808 feet: 20h 56m 59s (real time 19h 50m), feeling good. Out on my own at my own pace, in Fully, a little sleepy, didn't eat well, awake and running well again in Champex. Later, the organization stopped me for an hour, and I finished at Mermoud's insistence, very unmotivated, disappointed and angry."

"February 9, 2015. Ski Mountaineering World Championships in Verbier. 1,925 meters, 1h 28m 12s. Felt great going up and down, in control. Fresh and sprightly. Calm on the descent. Top form."

What seems important today, unlike when I started out as an athlete, is to become as fast a professional runner as possible, or proclaim the intensity of your training to the four winds so someone will believe in you. Before, you may have worked in the shadows and it was easy to be rigorous and honest and set yourself realistic goals that were appropriate for your level at a given moment. You trained and trained, and waited for your body to mature, so that maybe after a few years you could win a race. If you didn't doubt yourself, your expectations could be too high, and if you didn't give yourself time to do the patient, hard work of an ant, you could end up being mightily disappointed (*las hostias pueden ser antológicas*).

These days, if you're a beginner, you have to choose between being a professional, elite runner, belonging to the glorious top five percent in the world, or being a running *influencer*. If you don't compete, training becomes a professional accessory, and you have to choose your activities for their visual, communicative, or inspirational appeal as well as their potential to grab the attention of an audience, even though they may have zero athletic draw. If you don't take this path, you should be aware that the road is long and the results aren't guaranteed. If you achieve success, it will be after many years of hard work, with no immediate gratification.

Mind you, these are both valid and interesting life paths. The important thing is to know what you want and are looking for, because although the superficial layers of these two ways of life may be similar, they're actually as different as night and day.

If you want to be an elite runner, you'll probably accumulate a lot of frustration along the way plus put in a lot of effort that will largely go unnoticed and result in few rewards. In the end, the most valuable prize will be bringing out the best in yourself. If this isn't enough of a reward, then it's best to leave it, because you won't see the point of dedicating your life to difficult, endless training in pursuit of perfection. You won't understand why you should suffer so many injuries, follow such a strict diet, and deprive yourself of so many things. And all this without being able to take a vacation, because the life you have chosen fills every hour of every day. For decades.

This is the case for some European athletes who abandon the

privilege of Western comforts when they're still young to live a low-profile life, free from distractions, in a spartan room at a high-performance center in Iten, in the Kenyan highlands. There, they lead a monastic existence. And all to hang on to the possibility of one day being in the spotlight and dazzling an audience in some competition. The price of chasing this dream is living in a faraway place and dedicating years to achieving it—years that are impossible to get back if things don't turn out as they planned.

When I think of all this, the image that comes to mind is of the Font-Romeu Hermitage, which is, metaphorically, my Kenyan Iten, an old monastery converted into college accommodations with simple rooms, no internet access, and limited cell phone reception, at the foot of the ski slopes. Today, whenever I think about the speed of the modern world, the excess of information, stimulation, and stupid distractions, and how all this affects my body, I still take off in my truck and hide away somewhere remote, where no one can find me if I don't want to be found, and devote myself for a few weeks to regaining control over the essential virtuous cycle of an athlete's life: eat, train, eat, train, and sleep. Nothing else.

In pre-internet society, it was still possible to seek long-term results in life. Today, it's practically impossible to find anyone who sets themselves a long-term goal without the certainty of attaining it, since in order to survive, we need our basic needs met. And without knowing exactly how we got here, we have ended up believing that we have far too many basic needs. We live in an era when the memory of a self-sufficient past still endures, when people grew their own food or hunted, built their own houses, and figured out ways to stay healthy. In that context, money wasn't much of a necessity. But this has no place in the unbridled capitalism of the present, when we are unaccustomed to distinguishing between the money we need for basic day-to-day survival and the money we want to use for pleasure. From this point of view, office or factory work isn't so different from what an athlete does who trains by running up and down mountains; the economic goal is the same. That's why we must decide if we want to earn a living with work that provides a dose of passion, or if we want to prostitute ourselves a little with some other job that we don't like as much but that fills our pockets. We don't generally think about this when we're sixteen or seventeen and have to choose how we want to live and how much money we need to do so. This is too bad.

As soon as I won my first world championship, sports brand representatives began to appear out of nowhere, offering me a range of products. When I kept winning competitions, those same people offered me money to keep training and competing. Logically, they made me happy and lifted a weight from my shoulders by solving the financial aspect of my life.

With time, and with the influence of social networks, all this changed significantly. Results have stopped being the most important thing. Before, an athlete won a competition and appeared in the traditional media, or won the applause of other runners and of the audience attending the race. Today, added to all this is what's known as, ahem, *content creation* and *social communication*.

As an athlete, I have always been driven by the single goal of performing as well as I can, of planning projects and setting myself challenges to overcome. This is compatible with being such a hopeless case: I don't know how to grow a garden, I don't know how to hunt, and please don't ask me to build a house. I'm too set in my ways and have interests that take me far away from that kind of utopian way of life. I travel, I pollute, I use the internet; I don't really like clothes, but we have to protect ourselves from the cold with something. I didn't have the balls to choose the life of a hermit, and I am willing to prostitute myself to a certain extent in exchange for the money I need to keep surviving and have a good time while pursuing my passions. This has distanced me somewhat from the virtuous eat-sleep-train routine, and I have done and continue to do other kinds of work, like appearing in audiovisual materials and various kinds of media and talking to people. But I've had the good luck to be able to choose whom I associate with, and I haven't been forced to link myself to companies whose values and projects I don't share or admire. I admit that today I earn more money than I need to live, but I can also guarantee that when the commitments that allow me to earn that money risk distracting me from training and improving my performance, I draw the line. Money won't give me back the time that could make me lose.

Though I may have pursued progress and constant exploration from the beginning of my career, I never stopped to think about what kind of runner I wanted to be. And this was essential for knowing what kind of training regimen I would have to follow in the long term.

Did I want to be a long-distance runner? Would I rather be a ski mountaineer? Maybe one who competed every week? Or would it be better to be one of those who put themselves to the test a couple of times a year, but with impeccable training? Before anything else, I had to ask myself what kind of runner I admired most: one who can run a marathon in just over two hours, like the Kenyan runner Eliud Kipchoge, or one who can compete in over twenty races a year at an extremely high level, like the Japanese runner Yuki Kawauchi? Jeez. If I thought about total performance, Kipchoge; if I focused on recovery, Kawauchi. A big dilemma.

I admire both of these runners; each of them is equally inspiring. But what about me? I like to perform to my full potential, but at the same time, I don't want this to be detrimental to the other aspects of my activities. How much do I want to risk quality to increase quantity? This question makes my head begin to spin. On one hand, I want to keep fighting to win ski-mountaineering races, like the Pierra Menta, the Fully Vertical Kilometer, a 100-mile Ultra-Trail, or the Zegama marathon, and I don't want to stop participating in some to focus on others. On the other hand, I can't avoid the fact that today's runners are more specialized, and I don't know if I can stay competitive in all these areas at the same time. Despite everything, my mind wanders freely, and I have realized that for the time being, I'm not as excited about competition as I used to be. I see it as a kind of training. Yes, but what am I training for? And it's tough to leave the throne explicitly so others can occupy it, because it's really nice to occupy it yourself.

AFTER THESE REFLECTIONS, I WENT BACK TO MY ROUTINE. ONE MORNING, just like I do every morning, I got up, put on my shorts and sneakers mechanically, and drank a glass of water. I wasn't especially excited for the coming Sunday's race. Not enough to torture my body for the three or four hours I'd planned. I put on my headphones and selected a playlist I'd titled "Training." I was mad at myself because I hadn't given enough recognition to the fact that I do what I love, that I'm able to run, surrounded by stunning landscapes. I let the music take my mind off the passage of time, listened to the lyrics to a Sopa de Cabra song, and started to jog.

Rivers of wounded
People run alone
Spitting their failure.

I kept running just out of inertia, without any goal. The song made me feel worse and worse, because I recognized myself in its lyrics.

As they cry
Out of anger and love
For a nonexistent name.

I will turn back
When I'm too far away
I will turn back
When it's already too late.

I reached the summit and stopped. I had planned to do three rapid ascents, since that's what I usually did this time of year, but I no longer saw the point. I realized something wasn't right: that clear vision I'd had of everything had disappeared. Even though I know that one life contains many, for me it's a tragedy that we keep living just one, when its time is up.

I descended calmly, moving my legs little by little, but my head moved too fast and it wouldn't stop spinning. I wondered: *What can give me the motivation to keep training so hard?* My legs again sped up out of inertia. I began to think I should go back to my origins, that I should recover what made me tick before I knew what it meant to train and compete.

Preparing the Attack on Everest

It's hard for me to think of climbing a mountain as heroic. I know it's easy to make it look that way. When you're at the foot of a great mountain with glaciers towering above you, rocks that come loose in the heat, and distances that seem unconquerable, it's easy to convince others that climbing it is a titanic feat requiring superhuman physical abilities and the courage of the gods. But—sorry to disappoint you—this isn't the reality. Climbing a mountain is just putting your life in danger to try to reach the summit, and then coming down again. Clearly, this puts you in a category closer to stupidity than to heroism.

No matter how many athletes pretend this isn't the case, coordinating their expeditions with fundraising campaigns for charity or raising awareness about a rare disease, there's nothing heroic about climbing a high peak in the Himalayas. In fact, it's a selfish enterprise. A dangerous and expensive leisure activity.

I've always been drawn to high mountains, but the classic expedition dynamic doesn't appeal to me. Having to spend two to three months in a tent at base camp, waiting for a window of good weather that will allow you to undertake the ascent, seems to me like a pointless waste of time. *Boredom* and *idleness* are the two words that best summarize life at base camp. To make things worse, your physical condition deteriorates and your motivation gets buried beneath the snow. Life at base camp is like being trapped in a mountainous paradise, a prisoner of rest between the walls of your tent. In an ocean of gray stone and a desert of white powder, surrounded by dry air and beneath a blue sky. Flanked by rocky mountains, with a river of cold water crossing this desert of powder and cutting its snaking path toward lower terrain, to feed the grass and a few bushes.

If I go upstream, I will find the slope marked by mounds of stone that rumple the terrain like a tattered blanket, and farther up, I will glimpse the ice of an immense glacier. The wind is constant as it rushes down from the mountains, escaping from the white peaks along the same route as the river. During one visit to Everest, there were four small tents and another larger one at the edge of the slope, all a sun-bleached shade of yellow. Inside the largest one, it was like being at a regular campsite, with four chairs and a thermos of tea. I listened to the wind whip the walls, and a movie image of a helicopter came to mind, its propellers turning as it approached and retreated in turn, but it wouldn't leave, like in a nightmare.

There was a book in front of me that I'd already read a couple of times, and I regretted having left all the others at home. The clock only told two times: six in the morning, when we would meet for breakfast, and six in the evening, when we would get together again for dinner. In between, there were no hours, there were no minutes, no seconds, only time that dragged on indefinitely. *So fucking boring.* I stared into the distance, hoping to find any distraction. I no longer had the keen, restless gaze of the first few days; now my eyes had been dried by the wind and reacted only to a previously unseen mountain I dreamed of climbing, a black dog roaming around with the same look in its eyes as me, a cloud formation that reminded me of the outline of another, identical cloud I had seen one fall afternoon at home.

Soon after arriving, I had seen Vivian Bruchez take a Coca-Cola can and scratch some figures onto it with a Swiss Army knife, and I'd laughed at him; a few days later, I had spent hours looking over the enormous pile of silvery sculptures growing higher and higher. There were simple ones (a face, a mountain with ski tracks) and more complex ones (a climber abseiling down a rock face with a rope, a harness, and even some ice axes cut out of the tin). As he sculpted in silence, our absent gazes forgot the passage of time.

I watched Vivian in the throes of artistic creation, and suddenly I noticed my clothes were making me itch. My merino wool underwear was starting to get worn out. They were almost new when I arrived, but in a few days, they had become frayed. When I packed only a couple of pairs for the expedition, thinking of keeping the weight under the baggage limit, I hadn't realized that washing them in highly mineralized glacial water and hanging them in the dry air would weaken the fibers. Yes, the hole in the crotch was inevitable, and now one of my balls hung out when I walked.

In my tent, I grabbed a pen and held it above the blank paper like a weapon. I had no ideas. In fact, I had only one: everything has been written, everything is plagiarism, we drive ourselves insane by repeating things over and over and

over; it's impossible to say anything new. I flipped through
the pages of the notebook that had been with me for years on
my travels and expeditions. I looked at the sketches I had done
of prototypes for climbing boots, tents that would give better
protection against the wind, and lightweight ice axes. I read
my annotations on the calendars, times and dates with details
of activities, a few thoughts, and phone numbers and contact
info for people I'd met at some camp, whom I never ended up
contacting. I paused at a page I had written in Alaska, when I
went to run the Mount Marathon race, only 5K long, which
leaves from Seward, at sea level, and goes up and down the
peak behind the town, with an almost 1,000-meter slope. I
remembered that on my way there I had wondered if it was
worth it to take such a long trip for such a short race, about
forty minutes. But it had ended up being one of the most interesting races I'd ever run.

*I'm sweating and the sweat streams down my face, gets
into my eyes and makes them sting. I can only see my
hands resting on my knees, pressing my legs to climb
faster, and if I look up, Rickey Gates's ass. I know there's
a steep slope of black dirt up ahead, and beyond that, the
summit, which we'll go halfway around. My heavy breathing forces me to keep looking down at my hands on my
legs.* Hey, Rickey, what's the rush? Couldn't we let up a
bit? *I think. But we don't slow down, and when it's my
turn to set the pace, I try to challenge him by going even
faster. I breathe hard and I run. My calf muscles will
never love me; I've been abusing them for years and now
they're more tense than a set of guitar strings. Between*

each breath, I wipe the sweat from my brow and eyes with my hand. I'll need to be able to keep my eyes wide open when I run down at full tilt among all these rocks. I reach the summit and only have time to open my lungs and take a gulp of air. And then the rock and roll begins. And it won't stop until the finish line. And I don't want to go down head over heels. And it will go on all night. They say here that laws exist but they were written in a far-off place. I'm from Europe, where trail running is just called trail *for short, and is drunk on its own success, and now the fresh air of Alaska penetrates the whole event. You have to run up and down until you bleed, and celebrate it intensely. That is all.*

When someone pontificates, they clearly do so to protect their work, and they do so perpetuating the standards by which it was shaped. This someone tries to convince future generations that in order to achieve excellence, they should follow the same rules. But it's 4:30 in the morning—it's always 4:30 in the morning, just like Charles Bukowski said. We're so absorbed in our own path, in our effort to concentrate on doing everything well, with a religious passion for our discipline, and a fear of the unknown, that we keep our eyes on the road, on our hands pushing our knees. And we don't realize we're following the rules of a man who ran a horse race on foot, or of one who climbed higher than 8,000 meters alone without oxygen, or one who decided to leave his pitons, ropes, and safety harness at home, to become one with the face of the mountain. We're following the rules of those who broke them. Maybe it's time to break the rules and erase the pages we've written, though sometimes the ink is so dry that it's hard to see the blank paper. The backpack of our experiences should be a tool kit full of resources, but all too often it's nothing but a dead weight that doesn't allow us to fly freely.

I got up and went out, ready to climb one of the nearby peaks. I didn't have permission to do so, and it was possible that I'd be so tired when I finished that my chances of reaching the summit I'd come there to conquer would be reduced. But I had no patience, and I hated wasting time.

My Home
Is the Mountain

There is no single landscape I can call mine. I cannot point and say, "That's my house, between the mountain path to the north and the valley to the south." There are many places where I feel more or less at home, but none that I consider completely mine.

I grew up in La Cerdanya in a refuge shared by mountaineers, skiers, and tourists passing through. I suppose that's why I ended up being a wanderer, since when I was young I already lived in a place that didn't truly belong to anyone.

Usually, *home* is associated with a physical space, whether that is a building, neighborhood, town, city, or country; sometimes all that comes to mind are the four walls of a room. *Home* is where, when you walk in the door, you recognize the smell of clean clothes, stir-fry, or the scent of a field of wheat. It's the light that shines through the window each night, casting familiar shadows. It's waking up in the morning and walking around without needing to turn on the light. For me, however, all of these feelings are scattered since my home is a collection of specific spaces that make me feel good when I'm in them. I walk around La Cerdanya and suddenly feel at home, but the illusion disappears in the blink of an eye. I go back to Chamonix and the smell of fall welcomes me—I feel at home, but the spell is soon broken. In Nepal, too, the relaxed feeling of home sometimes takes hold of me for a moment. I can often feel more like I'm in my own place in some unknown country than when I'm in the house I've paid for and made my own, where some days I feel like a total stranger.

Maybe *home* is spending time with the people you love. *Home* is laughter. *Home* is making love, feeling the comfort of solitude, and crying without worrying that anyone else can see you. When I think of the little pieces of the world that make up my own, I realize there's one common denominator: they're all in the mountains.

The origin of all my headaches was having left home. The races are like cities, with all the people and noise. They end up becoming my habitual landscape. And I feel like a stranger.

I HAVE ALWAYS FOUND SERENITY IN SOLITUDE. FOR ME, THREE IS A crowd. As much with family as among friends, I have always felt like the person who has one foot in and one foot out. Like someone who feels at ease for a moment, every once in a while. In a world that is so connected and so *social*, I have never wanted to belong to any tribe.

When I was little, I thought that when I grew up I would

live in a remote, isolated house in the mountains, where it would take at least an hour to get to any inhabited place. I sketched out the plans and everything: one room to sleep in, another to store my sports equipment, and a kitchen with a table. Since I would be surrounded by nature, I wouldn't need a bathroom in which to hide from people; I could enjoy doing my business while gazing at magnificent views—far more inspiring than a white-tiled wall.

My childhood dreams are at odds with the reality of Chamonix, where I lived a big part of my life during the 2010s. For reasons of size and diversity, the men and women there gather according to their sense of belonging to a tribe, and being part of a group makes them think that some are better than others. Without my having asked, I was included in the gang of *Ultra-Trailers*. Though I never picked up my membership card, I also never bothered to try to remove the label that was given to me. I was too thirsty for activity, and except for the occasional time when I gave in to the insistence of a sponsor or journalist, I had never set foot in any bar, restaurant, or other place where people tend to meet to talk and confirm they belong to the tribe of chosen ones, something they show by the way they speak and dress and the places they choose to frequent.

I went to live in Chamonix in 2010 because, for me, it was a mythical place. When I was little, I'd already read many stories about it. It isn't a remote spot. On the contrary: it's in the middle of the Alps and very well connected. For me then, it was a symbolic space that allowed me to have adventures and progress in the world of mountaineering—perfect for recovering my connection to the mountains.

I CLIMBED MONT BLANC FOR THE FIRST TIME AS A TEENAGER, AND THE small satisfaction of reaching the summit didn't make up for what I had to do to achieve it. It was horrible. The first day, we climbed as far as the refuge, with extremely stiff boots and over-stuffed backpacks, and tried to sleep through the tractor-like snores of dozens of mountaineers. It was freezing cold when we left soon after midnight, and every few minutes we had to stop because someone in the group was tired or wanted to drink, eat, or take a photo. We arrived at dawn. The descent was even worse: it was hot, my feet were squashed in my boots, and on top of that, my back was aching. We looked like soldiers coming back from war, when at the end of the day all we had done was climb a mountain.

During those years, I went with my mother and sister to the Écrins region in the southern French Alps. We set up base camp at a site where we were staying, and from there we went out to do our activities: biking, running, or climbing. I learned that one of the most powerful runners of the time had left from that same campsite to ascend the Dôme de Neige, 4,000 meters, in the record time of three hours. I was only sixteen and had little experience, and this information gave me the incentive to climb it faster.

It was during one of those trips to the Écrins that I began to realize what kind of mountain I like to climb. I wasn't drawn to difficulty since it seemed too slow; classic mountaineering seemed too laborious. Racing and ski mountaineering are both activities I love but in which I miss the spirit of discovery and adventure. Continuous movement on technical terrain, though, gives me enormous enjoyment, in an unusual way. The French mountaineer Georges Livanos said that the essential thing wasn't to climb at a high speed but to climb for a long time. While I agree with the second part of this statement, if you climb at a high speed *and* for a long time, you can see much more. What made me fall in love with traversing mountains at high speed is the synergy that emerges between the body's movement and the shapes of nature, the feeling it gives me of being naked and inconsequential, unrestrained. It brings me freedom and connection, something I can't find if I go to the mountains any other way. At the same time, when it comes to making certain decisions, it creates a very fine line between the conscious acceptance of certain risks and stupidity. And I can say that I have sometimes crossed that line.

Let me tell you about it.

NIGHT WAS FALLING AND IT WAS SNOWING HEAVILY—AN INTENSE, ICY storm with lightning. Emelie and I were 50 meters from the summit of Aiguille du Midi, so close we could almost touch it with the tips of our fingers, yet so far because we were blocked by a wall of stone that made it impossible for us to go on. Emelie hadn't been able to feel her feet for a while, and her arms were stiff. The cold had contracted her muscles, and she couldn't open her hands. She sobbed as she breathed. She told me as best she could that she couldn't take any more, that she was suffocating. That she was going to die there. Though I knew that wasn't going to happen, that we would survive, I understood how hard it is to keep your cool when you're having an anxiety attack and trapped by a wall in the midst of a snowstorm with thunder and lightning, and daylight fading. Yes, I had screwed up. Really screwed up.

I held her face in my hands, covering her nose and mouth to limit her airflow. I felt the air push through my fingers, and she had to force her lungs to find it. Her breaths became longer and increasingly regular, and finally recovered their rhythm. But her feet and hands were too painful and seized up for her to go on. We had only a few feet of rope to descend the almost 1,000 meters we had climbed.

It was such a bad idea to involve Emelie in that climb. I knew bad weather was on its way; that was exactly why I had instigated the expedition, to get it done before it was too late and avoid having to wait a few weeks for the storm to clear. That's why I had thought it was better to go as soon as possible.

We had left at a leisurely pace that morning—there was no need to get up too early. At the beginning of the ascent I checked the weather for the last time: it looked like the front coming in from the south would arrive late in the evening, and that gave us time to climb up to the summit and back down into the valley.

The conditions for the climb were excellent. The warmth and good weather of the previous week had left the rock dry with excellent adherence, and we completed two-thirds of the route at a good pace, with no sign of any ice or snow. But when we reached the last stretch, everything changed. The sun had dried out the rock and melted the snow that covered the permanent ice—black, ancient, as hard as the granite it encased—and this required more skill and the use of crampons so as not to slip down. Almost from the start, Emelie's feet were hurting, after a summer of many punishing races. Tightening the rope to its limit, we began to climb confidently, little by little, until we had to stop because everything hurt, and then we went on a few meters up the rock.

We hadn't wasted much time, but the bad weather was clearly going to catch up with us soon. I looked for a way out over the rocks so we wouldn't have to step on the ice, and we kept going gradually, until finally the storm arrived. Along with the hail and lightning, our panic and distress. We took cover for a moment to see if it would ease off, but all signs pointed to the opposite. As we waited, the cold seeped into our bones, since we weren't wearing warm enough clothes. I kept climbing cautiously, but the pain in her feet meant Emelie couldn't go on. I weighed our options. We were anxious and shaking. *Fuck! How could I be so stupid?* Maybe I could climb those remaining 50 meters and tighten the rope to pull Emelie up, but I hadn't packed the three pieces I needed to make a hoist. We could shelter under a rock and wait until the next day, but I didn't have a cover for a bivouac, and Emelie didn't think we'd survive a night without cover with what little equipment I'd told her to bring. That was when I made the decision. I took out the phone and dialed the number of the PGHM, the Peloton de Gendarmerie de Haute Montagne—the French Alps emergency rescue team. As I did so, I was already starting to think about what that call would mean.

Although I thought the people in Chamonix who'd always criticized me for traveling so light would crucify me, I understood that their comments would be constructive and would show my followers that the mountains are full of risks, and that strength is no substitute for knowledge and preparation. In the end, the only thing harmed by the criticism was my ego.

I had to face up to my mistakes. The first was miscalculating what to take with me; you can get through tough situations with ingenuity and cold blood, but you still know you're going to have a shitty time. The second was assuming Emelie shared my view that the expedition was more important than our safety, and not predicting that she would feel uncomfortable in the situation we ended up in; in that sense, we were different.

I have never doubted that Emelie is smarter than me, because she prioritizes safety over her goals. She is capable of giving up much sooner than I am, whereas I don't hesitate to cross the red line of risk, knowing the conditions will be difficult to confront. On that climb, I should have been able to say "Enough" and leave it there. I shouldn't have made decisions as if I were climbing alone. We should have turned back before attacking the ice. The outing wasn't fun anymore, and it wasn't necessary to suffer so much.

I MET TANCRÈDE 2,000 METERS UP A WALL OF LE BRÉVENT, WHERE HE and a group of artist friends had set up a rope between two rock faces with a gap between them over 30 meters wide. There were acrobats, mountaineers, climbers, musicians—quite a group. They had proposed the game of walking along the rope, from one end to the other. It was an exercise in balance and concentration; you had to balance your body and arms to compensate for the swaying. This activity is called slacklining. It's most fun when done between two rock faces at a great height rather than between two trees in a park. It gives you a feeling of being above a total void. Even though we wore harnesses at Le Brévent in case we lost our balance, the feeling of emptiness around us was absolute. We were so gripped by the desire not to fall that we ended up ignoring everything we'd learned about balance, and in the end we fell easily.

When you're climbing or extreme skiing, two activities that allow for no errors, you never experience this sense of the void, since you never lose sight of the sky or the ground. But with high slacklining, everything is sky. I tried to walk that rope half a dozen times and only managed to take a couple of steps. Then Tancrède would patiently explain how I needed to empty my mind, how I should position myself. One day, without saying a word, he took off his harness, left it on the ground, and began walking along the rope. He reached the other side after crossing the hundred feet, turned around, and walked back the other way. The silence was absolute. There wasn't a sound. The musicians had put down their instruments; the climbers were quiet. We watched him in silence, glancing at him almost sideways, with the feeling that we were intruding in a private, intimate space.

He approached sport like an art, like a way to achieve symbiosis between the aesthetics of an activity and the nature surrounding it. It wasn't unusual to see him dressed up as a clown, wearing a parachute, or playing the violin as he crossed a rope stretched between two spires, up among glaciers of 3,000 meters, or dancing around with gymnastics ribbons on a 1,000-meter mountain face in the Norwegian fjords. He managed to take his art as far as it could go. He trained his body, watched his diet down to every last detail, and knew what every muscle was for. He prepared himself mentally, studying the activities he designed, his body weight, the force of the air, the acceleration of gravity, the distance of the fall, or the rate of gliding according to the body's surface, all from a scientific point of view. He had studied it all and was highly aware of his abilities. But there is a world of difference between knowing and doing. He was one of the best I have ever known. Yes, he was afraid of falling, but he knew how to break the barriers we build, to distinguish only what was real and definitive.

He made his body do unimaginable things—*jusqu'au bout*, as they say in French: "until the end." Tancrède was without a doubt a *jusqu'au-boutiste*.

SOME CLIMBERS LOOK DOWN ON OTHER MOUNTAIN SPORTS, THINKING their practitioners care only about the stopwatch. For them, mountaineering has a significant romantic component, with hardly any connotation of sport. The idea of the sport as a race against time makes them break out in a rash.

On the other hand, mountaineering can also be seen as extremely results-driven since it's based on a binary: summit or no summit, gear or no gear, yes or no, success or failure. Like other sports, it requires some parameters to establish whether or not the bar is being raised. The competition guidelines apply equally. Would any mountaineer deny having felt immense satisfaction and inner joy when learning he or she had reached a summit faster than anyone else? I don't think so.

The stopwatch is a companion that tells you you're doing well, that you're getting the best you can out of yourself. Though time may not be the ultimate goal, this little device whispers into your ear whether you're getting better or worse,

whether you're going strong or flagging, or whether you're being efficient when it comes to solving a problem. The stopwatch
doesn't lie.

IN THREE SPORTS AS DIFFERENT AS RUNNING, MOUNTAINEERING, AND
climbing, there is a common border, a shared measurement: the
two-hour threshold. Yes, the figure is anecdotal and arbitrary,
but runners, mountaineers, and climbers all have it seared into
their brains.

In running, the marathon is the queen of all competitions.
For the last few years, the best athletes have tried to outdo each
other by running the 26.22 miles in under two hours. For a while
now, efforts to achieve this magic number have heightened, and
the combination of factors that can help achieve it is studied
closely: young athletes with extraordinary physiological capacity are sought out and subjected to personalized training programs optimized for distance running; the ideal diet and
hydration before and during the race is studied; special sneakers
that help the runner lose the minimum amount of energy are
designed; biomechanics and efficiency of pace are assessed, even
the ideal temperature and humidity are taken into consideration.
After years of effort filing all the details, Eliud Kipchoge managed to break this two-hour barrier in 2019.

IN MOUNTAINEERING, THE TOUCHSTONE IS THE NORTH FACE OF THE
Eiger, in the Alps. In 1938, German mountaineers Anderl Heckmair, Heinrich Harrer, Fritz Kasparek, and Ludwig Vörg climbed

that 1,500-meter slope on a 3-kilometer expedition, with difficulty, in three days. Since then, it's been the ultimate challenge for mountaineers. Those among the elite can open up new and difficult paths to put their abilities to the test, either in a rope team or alone. Though these climbs present considerable risks, since any mistake can mean a potentially deadly fall, mountain climbers have used the wall at Eiger to explore new training methods, equipment, and strategies. In addition, Eiger has provided the opportunity to explore new limits, not only technical and physical limits but also in the acceptance of compromise. As the years went by, the ascent time was gradually reduced: Michel Darbellay was the first to take eighteen hours alone; Reinhold Messner and Peter Habeler arrived in ten; and Ueli Bürer, Franček Knez, and Thomas Bubendorfer brought the time down to less than five. In recent years, Christoph Hainz, Dani Arnold, and Ueli Steck have completed the climb in less than two and a half hours. The two-hour horizon is getting closer and closer. As it approaches, greater and greater risks are assumed.

The trilogy of two-hour climbs is completed by the ultimate climb up El Capitán in Yosemite Valley, California, by the most mythic route of The Nose, at 880 vertical meters. The first to climb it were the Americans Wayne Merry and George Whitmore, in an incredible forty-seven days. From that moment on, climbing El Capitán in just one day became a dream that remains impossible for the majority. But in 1975, the dream was achieved by Jim Bridwell, John Long, and Billy Westbay—three of the most innovative climbers in history. Those who came after have perfected the technique and optimized the materials, reducing the time further and further. While the risks presented by speed aren't as great as with the Eiger, and physical ability is less of a determining factor than for a marathon, speed and resistance are the key to achieving the goal, along with logistical optimization and the ability to visualize every movement of the almost 1,000-meter climb. Rope teams had come close to the mythical two hours in previous years, until finally Alex Honnold and Tommy Caldwell managed it after months of targeted training, taking the route dozens of times.

These three examples can't be compared in any way. More than a million people run marathons every year, and of these, approximately a thousand compete. Around two hundred climb The Nose, and those who climb the north face of the Eiger number less than a hundred. Nor are they comparable in terms of risk.

However, they share one very important factor: in each of these disciplines, the athletes are motivated to conquer the arbitrary fact of *time*, and have had to find the inner and outer abilities they lacked in order to triumph. With this goal on the horizon, they prepared to the extreme to show what a talented human being can do, with hard work and discipline. And by pursuing it, they gave us all a gift, by offering us the tools to find motivation in each of our daily tasks.

IN THE MOUNTAINS, THE IDEA OF A RECORD IS RELATIVE, SINCE IT'S impossible to compare two times even on the same peak. In track and field, for example, a record has to be set on a track or circuit that guarantees certain conditions (wind, terrain, etc.) and parameters that leave no room to doubt equal opportunity (anti-doping tests, identical aid and provisioning for all participants, etc.). But this is impossible in the mountains, since conditions vary day by day and everyone climbs in a different way. That's why it's impossible to speak of records in this field; instead, performance is measured by *fastest known time*. In any case, I believe the comparison should be individual, since this allows you to know yourself and to know how fast you can cover terrain, taking into account the difficulty, distance, and conditions. It's impossible to equate the time of a runner who knows the route like the palm of his or her hand with that of one attempting it for the first time, or compare the time of one who attempts it with no assistance (a team of climbers, oxygen tanks, climbing ropes, etc.) with that of another who has the support of a team and resources.

A journalist may emphasize and value the time achieved, but in the end, speed should be less important than an athlete's inner assessment of his performance. And this has to do with his own evaluation of the results of his training and preparation, and the conditions under which he or she has achieved this concrete time.

Four basic factors give rise to improvements in time. The first is personal performance, where physical ability, technique, the economy of the race, experience, strategy, and psychological state all play a part. The second is the optimization of the route, in other words, whether you know the difficulties, whether you know the movements, and where you can cut them down. The third is the conditions, given that it's not the same to practice in bad winter weather as on a sunny summer day. The fourth is the kind of ethic you want to apply, which includes the question of going with or without assistance, alone or in company, the kind of equipment you use, or even whether or not to resort to doping, whether this be mechanical or physiological.

The case of Ueli Steck on the Eiger is a good example. He knew the route perfectly, and with painstaking preparation he was able to make the climb in two hours twenty-two minutes, with the line marked and hanging on to two fixed ropes at a couple of crossings. He also made the climb more slowly, in two hours forty-seven minutes, but with no trail to guide him on the mountain, and free-climbing all the passes. In other words, without touching the available ropes. Which of these records is better? Of course, the climb completed in the least time is the most attention-grabbing, but the other is probably harder to achieve, since it implies more physical work and commitment. In any case, both times are equally interesting because they show you what you can do under different conditions, without losing sight of the fact that time is not the only important thing but rather just one of the fruits of an equation in which each factor plays a determining role.

I WAS HEADING DOWN THE VALLEY ROAD TO RAUMA AND HAD DRIVEN nonstop for over thirty hours since setting out from Chamonix. The truck was loaded with all of my and Emelie's possessions. I wanted to get to the place where we'd decided to live together as soon as possible, and by now my eyelids had been heavy for hours. Dawn was breaking when I went through the wide ravine, along a road flanked by rock faces over 1,000 meters high. The daylight still wasn't bright enough to show the textures, but I could just see the endless dark rock spurs and the frigid waterfalls gushing down into the valley. It was like entering a land that didn't belong to human beings. The vertical walls of dark, slick rock were so close together that I couldn't see them in the distance. Finally, as I continued to drive while trying my best to fight off sleep, I saw it, lit by the faint light: a fine line of snow that, like a drop of water, seemed to trickle vertically down the middle of the wall. She called to me, and though at the time her voice gave me a chill, I knew one day I wouldn't be able to resist her call.

Three years later, I was still falling in love with her melody as I stole glances at her, and even sometimes awoke dreaming of her voice. I had been studying her all that time from the distance of the surrounding peaks, or touching her feet. Until the time came to sing the song with her up close.

For months I watched the line that had dazzled me when I passed through the gorge the Rauma River cuts through, the Norwegian valley of Romsdal. I studied it from different angles—from the foot of the wall, from its summit, and from the surrounding peaks—wondering which part I could ski and which outcroppings of rock or ice I would have to skirt. Then for two years I studied the conditions of the snow, and from time to time I observed how it adhered to the wall: when it stayed stuck, when it was too cold, when it looked good on the high *and* low parts of the mountain. Sometimes when I finished training, I took a detour on my way home to a point where I had a good view of the wall, and I observed it through binoculars or I took photos with a zoom lens to study later. I wondered what kind of skiing I could do, which equipment I would need, and what difficulties I would face. This phase of the study is almost as exciting as the expedition itself, since while

I'm planning, I close my eyes and imagine all the details in my head. I can almost feel the cold on my face or the pain in my hands, or the shiver that runs down my spine when I see myself do a turn with my skis in the air. I also anticipate everything that could go wrong: an avalanche, slipping on ice beneath the snow, or messing up a turn. I often postpone expeditions because my anxiety about them is physical, I don't know if I can accept the risk or the pressure, or on the day I plan to leave, my whole body is filled with a strange malaise. When I finally take it on, I know I've examined all the risks.

The third winter I spent in Norway, the wind seemed to blow in my favor. It was a magnificent winter, with plenty of snow, but without excessive quantities of precipitation, followed by long periods of sun, which allowed the snow to stick well to the wall, and without enough volume to trigger avalanches on the slope. The main problem was presented by the line to the right of the Troll Wall, which basically traverses the first climbing route on the north wall of the Trolltind, called Fiva: within the vertical mile that ends almost at sea level, there is a wide range of conditions. In the lower 2,000 feet, the snow is affected by temperature changes and humidity, while in the upper 3,000 feet, the environment is more alpine.

During the past weeks I had gone to the foot of the wall a couple of times and climbed the first 200 meters to get a real idea of what it was like from inside. Though the snow was harder than desirable, the conditions were almost perfect since the ski line was completely covered with snow, and it seemed like the high part of the route wouldn't accumulate a dangerous amount.

Then came the worst moment before a project bears fruit: the wait and choosing the day. Today? Tomorrow? Next week? If I always awaited ideal conditions I'd never get up from my couch. In incline skiing, it's best to ski on hard snow, which doesn't allow for error but is more stable than powder; in powder you can be less precise, but an avalanche can strike when you least expect it. In this kind of skiing, finding a balance between your movements as you descend and adherence to the wall is key.

And the day arrived. The first turn is always the most difficult—not because it's the most exposed but because it's difficult to take a step into the unknown. Your heart pounds in your chest, there's a pit in your stomach, your feet are sweating, your hands are, too. I drove a pole under my skis and felt the snow's texture through it. I observed the whiteness and moved the point forward to where I would break my turn, trying to guess with my eyes what the snow was hiding beneath it. I slid the skis back and forth quickly, letting my body move forward a few inches. I leaned my weight on the tips of my skis and gained momentum. A lot. I inhaled as much as I could and began to exhale but cut it short. My heart stopped, my breathing stopped, and I was suspended above, motionless and eternal. Suddenly I felt the skis touch the snow again; now they slid softly, gaining speed, pressed against the sixty-degree slope. My legs strained, and I felt like the skis were warping as they embraced the snow, first gently, then with more momentum, until they scratched and tore through it and, little by little, turned to land at a right angle, and I came to a stop with a sharp movement, a couple of meters below where I had begun the turn. A mixture of excitement and fear, pleasure and hesitation ran through my veins, and would stay with me turn after turn as I descended, following the footprints I had left on my way up. I dodged the patches of ice and rock dotting the snow, which in the next two hours would force me to get the best out of myself. I put all the training and techniques I had at my disposal into practice, and with every meter I gained, my hesitation gave way to pleasure, and my fear to satisfaction. Finally, when I got to the bottom, I turned back. I looked up at the tracks the skis had left on the wall of snow. And all the feelings surged through me, from my feet to my stomach. And my chest. And my head. A genuine orgasm of adrenaline.

I DON'T THINK THERE'S A BEST OR WORST STYLE—OR WAY—TO CLIMB A mountain. The purest way is almost impossible, due to our limitations as a species in the natural world. Michael Reardon, one of the most prolific solitary climbers ever, said that if you set out barefoot, without knowing the way, and without any chalk or rope, you can consider yourself to be climbing; everything else is commitment. And each and every one of us lives with this commitment. Our ethics are the rules we impose on ourselves and apply to the actions we carry out, but they relate to the ethics of each individual; we do not impose them on others. While commitment is identical for everyone when it comes to races— and even then, there are judges, referees, and tests to make sure everything is in order—in mountain expeditions, the decision should be an internal, personal one.

THERE IS ONLY ONE RAPID ASCENT I CAN SAY I'M ABSOLUTELY PROUD of, for having achieved total optimization. This is the Cervino ascent. Maybe it's because when I was little, I had an enormous poster of this mountain in my room, or because the time in which Bruno Brunod had climbed it (three hours fourteen minutes) seemed like a dream, one I believed impossible to achieve. The ascent is a beautiful one, and I mustered enough motivation and patience to prepare for it.

On August 1, 2013, I took my truck and headed to Cervinia in the Aosta Valley, and settled into the slope that unfolds at the foot of Cervino—Matterhorn. I had no particular date in mind to attempt the climb and no pressure to do so before moving on to other projects. For two weeks, I went to the summit almost every day, regardless of conditions, to get to know the mountain well, to see how the sun's heat affected the stone it fell on by the hour, and to interiorize each of the movements I had to make to follow my path. In short, to get to know it until I had made it my home and felt like a part of it.

Every morning I got up and watched the mountain from the truck window while I had breakfast, assessing any changes in the conditions of the snow and rock. At the same time, I sensed my body preparing itself. Even on the eve of the Sierre-Zinal race, which took place on the northern face of the mountain, I went up to the summit. At that moment, I wasn't interested in any competition result or future project. The only thing on my mind was preparing myself to the maximum and waiting for the ideal conditions.

On August 21, I felt like my body's condition and the conditions on the mountain had aligned. It hadn't rained or snowed for days, the rock was dry, the weather warm, and after nine ascents in the previous two weeks, I knew the route perfectly and was both physically and mentally prepared. I waited until the afternoon to avoid running into anyone on the mountain, and for the sun to have melted the ice from the night before and the rock to have more grip. When the bells chimed three, I left the bell tower's shadow and carried out each movement to climb up and down the mountain in two hours fifty-two minutes, just as I'd planned.

UNFORTUNATELY, I CAN'T SAY THE SAME FOR THE OTHER PEAKS I'VE climbed with the same intention of climbing them fast. I have not prepared as much or given them so much effort. I've always tried to do as well as I can, seeking the best conditions, but have never had the patience to wait more days than planned for them to be optimal. I've never worked so hard on a route that I made it "mine," or been vigilant enough for my physical and mental condition to be one hundred percent. Of course, this isn't to say that I'm not proud. While on Cervino, I learned to use the tools necessary to reach the summit as fast as my abilities allowed; in my other ascents, I didn't want to waste so much time preparing or seeking that level of detail. I learned to go fast, even when I was in poor condition, like when I climbed Denali while feeling unwell—with no assistance and struggling against myself, I found out how far my body could go when it was rebelling. In all of my climbs, I have gotten to know myself better, and to know how fast I can go in different circumstances and with different levels of preparation.

I'm too impatient. I don't know if that's a virtue. I admire the approach of those who work hard on details, but I would never make the sacrifice to set a spectacular record or win a victory for the ages if I had to spend a year without doing anything else to achieve it. For example, my perfect fortnight was in July 2015. I began with an extreme ski descent of Mont Maudit and went on through a couple of days of nonstop activity in the Grandes Jorasses. After that, I did a vertical 1K race in Chamonix, then squeezed in a photo session that night with a sponsor, and the next morning accompanied Karl Egloff to help him try to break the time-to-ascend record of Mont Blanc, which I had set with Mathéo Jacquemoud two years earlier. The idea was to take it at a good pace along the paths and shortcuts I knew for 1 or 2 kilometers of slope until he began to get away from me, but since I'd been feeling good from the beginning, we went all the way to the summit together. Even though the snow conditions weren't ideal and Karl wasn't feeling great, we made it up and down in just over five and a half hours. That same night, Emelie and I went to the United States, first to run the Mount Marathon in Alaska and five days later the Hardrock 100 in Colorado.

I BELIEVE YOU ONLY LIVE ONCE AND YOU HAVE TO MAKE THE MOST OF every second. I guess this impatience has led me down a self-taught path since usually, when I have wanted to go out and do some activity, I have never wanted to wait for a friend to be free or to expand my circle of acquaintances by going with someone new. So, my solution has been to go alone and learn by following the patterns of my mistakes and successes. That's how I climbed my first routes over ice and rock, and how I completed the majority of my ascents. It's a slower path than if you climb with friends or mentors, because with certain challenges you need a clear idea of the risks and shouldn't doubt your abilities. When you go it alone, you integrate and consolidate what you learn more concretely, and you have to rely solely on your imagination to escape difficulties.

Though I also have to admit that there comes a point where you can't go any farther alone . . .

EVEREST IN
SUMMER

When I arrived in Rongbuk, I jumped out of the car and observed the mass of tents at the Everest base camp. Until then, I had always gone to the Himalayas in the off-season and had always been able to enjoy the solitude. That's why, as I sat in my seat, my eyes almost popped out of my head at the small city of tents of every size and color that made up the camp. I could hear voices speaking in many languages and smell food cooked with African spices and olive oil. I got out of the vehicle that had brought me from nearby Cho Oyu, where I had been with Emelie all those months ago, and wandered around until I found Sébastien Montaz's tent. My eyes weren't yet accustomed to the landscape, which looked halfway between mountain and city. What I had seen eight months earlier, when I had been here for the first time, was still engraved on my memory.

IT WAS THE MIDDLE OF AUGUST 2016. WE HAD ARRIVED AT RONGBUK after two weeks, during which the agency we'd hired in Lhasa, the center of Tibetan Buddhism, to set up logistics on the mountain—a tent with a kitchen and eating area, a month's worth of food, a cook, and the air and car trips from Nepal to Tibet—drove us a little crazier than we'd expected. They showed up with a new problem every day, and it wasn't clear when we would finally leave. In the end, we were so fed up that one day we ran out of patience and went to the nearby Langtang Valley to let off some steam and escape the polluted city air. After a week—*About time!*—we could finally leave for Tibet in search of the thin mountain air we longed for.

The journey to Rongbuk is incredible. The magnificent Buddhist temples of cities like Xigatse, in immaculate shades of white and gold, contrast with the surrounding parched landscape and the Tibetan Plateau's endless miles of savannah, at an altitude of about 5,000 meters. The monotony of the land's gentle undulations is interrupted only by its great lakes and the rivers that cross it. Strings of eye-catching prayer flags announce the proximity of a village.

The road that crosses this region is perfectly paved, and after a few hours, we left the plain behind. The landscape's undulations became more pronounced before we reached the top of a hill and the magnificent ridge of the Himalayas appeared. An impassable barrier of white giants rising out of a brown and yellow plain. Straight from the flatlands to 8,000 meters. To the left, Makalu and Chomo Lonzo; to the right, Cho Oyu and Gyachung Kang; and in the middle, making its neighbors look puny by comparison, stands Everest. Between the rocky Kangshung wall of Lhotse and the snowy north wall of Nuptse, a perfectly proportioned triangle is drawn on the sky, painted white by the summer snows, with two parallel lines cut into it, dropping directly from the summit to the valley, the Norton and Hornbein Couloirs.

We were eager to merge with that white ocean, but before going into the valleys we had to stay a few more days in Tingri, one of the last villages before base camp. We always had to wait until tomorrow, even though we didn't know what we were waiting for. When we finally managed to get to base camp, twenty days after leaving home, the impatience to get moving and go up the mountain was eating away at me. It was August 20, the same day Reinhold Messner had ascended alone and without oxygen in 1980, up this same slope, in the midst of a monsoon.

We had arrived two weeks later than anticipated, feeling like we'd been wasting our time, and got to work straightaway to speed up our acclimation. No sooner had we arrived than I ran up to a peak 6,600 meters from base camp, and the next day, taking advantage of the summer heat, 7,000 meters up the North Col, in sneakers. The sun had softened the snow, and I managed to slide down on the soles of my shoes as if they were skis. I wanted to go out running or climbing every day, to put my physical state to the test, but Jordi Tosas wouldn't stop telling me:

"Be careful! It's normal to be nervous and want to do more than necessary and go up quickly at the beginning of an expedition, but everything's going to be decided in just two days at the end, and then you'll need to have your batteries charged. You need to act like a sniper and not get stressed before it's time."

WHEN YOU PREPARE FOR AN EXPEDITION, IT'S IMPORTANT TO GATHER the maximum amount of information before planning an assault on the summit. But there's no need to exaggerate. If you spend too much of the day studying the weather and waiting for the perfect conditions, you'll end up thinking that opportunities are passing you by, and that maybe you should take a risk every now and then and go on up. It's difficult to achieve perfection both in your performance and in the conditions. In the end, you have to learn to set out without worrying so much and struggle along with whatever you get.

We had been set up on the mountain for a week, and the forecasts agreed that there were only three or four days of good weather left before a storm took hold on the north face of Everest again, and if we didn't make the most of that window, we'd have to wait until the snows passed and twiddle our thumbs for another week until good weather left the mountain in acceptable shape. Otherwise, attempting it would be suicide, climbing in a minefield of avalanches. In the Himalayas in summer, you can believe the weather forecast if you want, but the algorithms aren't too precise when it comes to determining how much snow will fall. You must trust your own daily observations of the sky.

We noticed we were waking to a blue sky bathed in sunlight practically every morning, and around midday, the clouds would begin their procession from the south and accumulate, building castles with enormous gray towers over the plains of Nepal. These fortresses would advance north until they collided with the highest peaks, exploding into storms. Sometimes, their rage was trained on the south face, and we had a great time applauding the fireworks of lightning on display for us at the camp, on the opposite slope of Everest. At other times, the clouds came to greet us, forcing us to wait in our tents until they passed, listening to the tap-tap of the snow against the walls. But it was rare for us to wake up in the morning and see more than 10 or 15 centimeters of fresh snow, which melted with the sun's morning visit.

Yet now the dark swirling clouds on the south face were getting ready to burst with full force on this side of the mountain. If Everest had to give us a dance, it should be before the light display of the storm began.

Our base camp was in the middle of a rocky moraine between Rongbuk and the Everest glacier. We had intended to pitch our tents at the foot of the mountain, but the yaks carrying our equipment had decided to leave us stranded halfway there. We set up the four tents on a rocky slope, clumsily trying to pile the rocks into flat platforms. The place was so spectacular it was overwhelming. The moraine we were in was very large, with peaks up ahead of 6,000 to 7,000 meters, and behind us, a small ring of other peaks of the same height that we could climb with our skis some afternoon when we were bored. If the tedium lasted longer, we could always ascend Changtse, a friendly mountain at 7,500 meters, and go up along its north slope, knowing this would offer an impeccable view of Everest.

The only disadvantage of our exceptional lookout point was that it was so far from the top of the world. Each morning we had to travel about 10 kilometers before reaching the glacier and starting to climb, and when we came back tired, we had to do the same in reverse. But at last we were on the mountain and could do something every day.

WE ASSUMED WE'D HAVE A WINDOW OF GOOD WEATHER FOR JUST A few days, so we decided to finish acclimating and try to attack the summit. The previous days had been intense, and my body seemed to be asking for a break, but I'm not very good at relaxing, and I agreed with Sébastien to do one last, high climb to finish off the acclimation before our definitive attempt.

After dinner, we agreed to get up at five in the morning to start the ascent and went to our tents to get some rest. I got my backpack ready and fell asleep like a log as soon as I got into my sleeping bag.

I awoke to the sun caressing my skin through the tent's translucent walls. This is one of the nicest morning feelings, when it's still cold outside and the first rays of light appear, getting trapped between the walls of the tent and turning it into a makeshift sauna after the inhospitable cold of the night before. But suddenly I was startled to realize that the sun shouldn't be up yet. My sense of well-being vanished. I looked for my watch among the clothes I used as a pillow. "Damn it, ten past six!" I leapt out of my sleeping bag and got dressed in a rush. I didn't even eat breakfast. I grabbed my backpack and literally set off running up the moraine. I don't know if it was the fright or the adrenaline, but in any case, all the tiredness I had built up disappeared, and I ran as fast as I could.

After half an hour, I was already halfway to the foot of the mountain, in half the time it usually took me. When the sun began to burn brightly, I slathered my face in sunscreen and, without stopping, looked for my sunglasses. I began to feel nervous because they weren't on my head, or in my pockets, or in my backpack, which I tipped out onto the ground in a rage like an evil beast. Nothing. No sign of my sunglasses. "Fucking hell!" Without even thinking about it, I left my backpack on the ground and ran down the moraine to the tent. No sooner had I opened the zipper than there they were. Seven sharp! As I was about to dart off again, Sitaram, the Nepalese cook who had accompanied us, stuck his head out of his tent.

"Breakfast, Kilian!"

"No way, I don't have time, Sitaram, I'm heading back up. See you this afternoon."

"Don't run—it's not good for you at this altitude!"

I didn't even have time to hear the last thing he said since I was already retracing the path I'd taken before. I kept going, this time with everything I needed.

About three hours later, I saw Séb a few hundred meters away, heading up the wall of Changtse toward the North Col.

"God damn it, next time you could wake me up!" I shouted, half joking and half serious, once I was close enough for him to hear. I felt great, but now it was late, and the snow was warming up very quickly.

"Oh, I thought you wanted to sleep a little more, and I knew you'd catch up with me anyway," he said. "What do you think?"

"I think we're too late. The sensations are good, but we shouldn't push our luck. We're going to need it later on! If we go down now we'll be able to rest, and tomorrow or the next day we can try again."

THE NEXT DAY, I WENT UP ALONE. MAYBE I WAS A LITTLE ASHAMED OF my mistake the day before, and mad that I hadn't been able to acclimate above 7,000 meters, so I set out determined to overcome that altitude. My companions stayed at the camp to save their energy. I had the whole mountain to myself, and I smiled with a certain amount of selfish possessiveness. When I reached the glacier, I decided not to head toward the North Col for fear of the crevasses and chose a line on the right side of the northeast face. Between the spurs of rock and seracs that crown the North Col, there was a corridor with a slope that seemed steep enough to have shed the accumulated snow but not to slow down my pace. I decided to cross it. The conditions were perfect and the snow easily supported my weight, and a few hours later I left the sixty-degree slopes and came out onto the north ridge at an altitude of 7,500 meters. The snow wasn't melting, and I found myself buried up to my waist.

Every step required immense effort and precise choreography: I began by flapping my arms like a butterfly's wings to remove the first layer of snow, then I lifted my foot to the height of my knee, planting it 30 centimeters ahead. As I watched it sink, I trod gently to compact the snow before putting all my weight on it. Sunk up to the waist again, I did the dance with my other leg. And so on, thirty times over.

It took me an hour to climb 100 meters. After three hours of forging my way by making a trench, I stopped, more exhausted by the slowness of the process than by the effort. I flattened the snow and sat down on my backpack. My eyes were overwhelmed by all the beauty as I sat there with Everest at my back and the Tibetan Plateau in front of me. Changtse had grown smaller, and the surrounding mountains competed to seduce me with their majesty. At their feet, the valleys sketched numerous glaciers that spread out like tentacles from the snowy peaks, then faded away into the brown hills. From that height, to my left, I could see clearly the tongue of snow emerge that Reinhold Messner had crossed to seek the Norton Couloir and reach the summit in 1980.

The silence was so perfect that my own breath seemed to

insult the peace. I stopped my lungs for half a minute and felt a part of all that surrounded me, that I had merged with the environment like a tiny, insignificant snowflake, one with the good fortune to have fallen on that mountain. A line zigzagged through the snow and disappeared where the glacier turned behind the mountains. It was a reminder that I was only passing through, that soon I would have to rejoin the human world. But I wanted that moment to go on forever, away from troubles, my only concern to breathe, so intoxicated by the altitude that I was free of thoughts.

THE SNOWFLAKES WERE LUCKY, THEY COULD STAY IN THAT WHITE paradise, suspended in time, but human imperfections—hunger, cold, tiredness—forced me down. At the camp, four people were waiting for me.

Forty hours later, on the last day of August, I was back there again, but this time the silence had dissolved and there was a sound so intense it was indescribable—the sound you may imagine of the scream in the painting by Edvard Munch. At an altitude of almost 8,000 meters, in the middle of the northeast wall of Everest, I wasn't sure we would make it out of there alive. A few minutes earlier, everything had been euphoria.

In the wee hours of that morning, Séb, Jordi, and I had left the camp knowing it would be one of the last days of good weather before a week of storms. We moved across the moraine in silence, each absorbed in our thoughts. Only the sound of our shoes making the frozen ground crack broke the early morning monotonous calm. As the sun roused itself in the east, we arrived at the glacier, where the multitude of platforms of stone and the leftovers from other expeditions showed us that a small city was established there every spring.

We stopped at that ghost camp. We put on our boots with crampons and ate a little while we admired the sun, which was painting layers of red on the wall where we planned to ascend. When dawn broke and the orb shone on us, it was as if it were bringing a flower back to life. We took off our hoods and moved our heads freely to get a better view of our surroundings, and began to debate the best place to begin our attack on the 2,000 meters of snow and rock that would welcome us.

Tic-tac, tic-tac, crampon, ice axe, crampon, ice axe. Just like two days earlier, the snow had a perfect consistency, neither too hard nor too deep, and we moved along at a healthy pace of 250 meters per hour. After just a few hours, we reached 7,000 meters, climbing up broad, snowy slopes punctuated by spurs of rock that rose up to the pinnacles of the Northeast Ridge, commonly known as the Boardman Tasker Ridge, higher than 8,300 meters.

As we climbed, we were suspended inside a euphoric bubble. When you climb alone, your concentration must always be absolute, and you do your best to calm your emotions so they won't control or betray you; but when you're with others, feelings flow and the smiles are contagious. We were full of joy. The weather was the best we could have imagined, it wasn't cold, and the conditions were ideal. The three of us were in shape, especially Séb, and we were opening a new route up Everest!

Séb and I took turns in the lead, and Jordi followed us a short way behind. We went through some snow corridors and continued along a spur with some rock jutting out but a lot of accumulated snow, and we had to shorten the turns we took. Every 30 or 40 meters we switched off cutting a path through the snow, which was getting deeper and deeper. In the west, clouds were surrounding Raphu La, the pass separating the northeast slopes and the Kangshung Face of Everest, and they began to envelop the wall we were climbing. All week, small clouds had begun to form in the early afternoon and soon disappeared, so we didn't feel daunted. Though we were at almost 8,000 meters, where breathing is laborious and it takes a huge effort to keep going, we were in the throes of euphoria, and while I went up ahead, cutting a path up to my knees, I heard Séb start singing, "*Libéré, délivré, je ne t'oublierai plus jamaaais . . . Libéré, délivré . . . ,*" a parody of the song from his daughters' favorite cartoon, the only movie we had access to at the camp.

We decided to stop and wait for the clouds to flee, but they refused. In fact, they did the exact opposite. They became denser and denser, until we couldn't see more than a dozen meters ahead. As if that weren't enough, it started snowing.

Our situation was precarious. The wind had begun to blow and now it was lashing us violently, and between the snow that was falling and the snow already accumulated, slabs of an alarming size had begun to form. We were right in the middle of a wall that could become an avalanche trap in a matter of hours, or even minutes. Séb's eyes met mine in the midst of the storm. There was no need to say anything more: it was impossible to go on.

We had only three choices: wait, go down the way we came, or find a new direction to head in. None of them inspired much confidence. We could go back the way we came about 500 meters with no serious technical complications, but the accumulated snow could be dangerous. Crossing to the right in search of the north ridge meant less of a risk, but to get there, we would have to cross a fifty-degree slope with over a meter of freshly accumulated snow. In those conditions, waiting didn't seem like a good idea.

When Jordi caught up with us, we asked him what he thought.

"I think we have to cross over diagonally toward the ridge," he said.

"I'm not crossing if I can't see where I'm going," replied Séb, trying to orient himself through the thick fog. "We can also go down really fast—that's another option."

Jordi tilted his head to one side before interjecting. "But there's the ice, and the ridges, and now they'll be completely loaded with snow."

"You can see the ridge now," I added, trying to mediate as I glimpsed its silhouette when the wind lifted the fog for a moment. "After the first spur there's another, and then there's the crest, about four or five hundred meters away."

"Okay," Séb agreed. "We'll go one at a time."

"All right, I'll go," I said, without thinking twice.

"Are you going because you don't have children?" Séb wanted to know.

"Yeah, that's part of it." My words had come out in a whisper. Immediately I began to walk.

I heard Séb's voice behind me. "When you get to the ridge, give a shout and we'll follow, eh?"

With each step I took, my body sank until the snow came up to my knees. Despite the crampons, my wide boots, ankle boots, and all the clothes I was wearing, I felt each millimeter of snow I crushed, the consistency of every crystal. When I felt a very hard layer of snow, I breathed relatively easily, at least until I began the next step, but when the layer sank suddenly, I held my breath for a few moments until I could tell everything was still. *One step more. I'm still crossing. I've stopped. Should I turn back?* If I turned back, I would just be postponing our fate. One more step. My knees disappeared beneath the snow. A thousand meters of wall above and a thousand below. All completely laden with snow. The wind was turning it into an enormous slab. *Fuck, this is a trap. It's a minefield!* With every step, I thought I would trigger an avalanche; I didn't know whether it would be 20 centimeters or a meter thick. Each movement was eternal, never-ending. When I stepped forward, before putting all my weight on my foot, I was already shaking at the thought of the next step. True, if I died I wouldn't be leaving that much behind, but . . . Emelie was on my mind and in my heart. We had planned a shared life together. I was also desperately counting the mountains I still hadn't climbed, which would remain in my head and never become a reality. I didn't want to die, not yet. I moved one foot forward and stopped again. I repeated the same process, with the same fear. Walking was hard, but the decision to take one more step was even harder.

"Aaaagh!!!" I cried at the top of my lungs as the snow that surrounded and supported me began to detach and slide down the wall.

Instinctively, I sank two ice axes as deeply as possible into the snow, scratching through each millimeter to find the ice beneath. A wave of snow crashed quickly onto my head from above, and I clung to the ice axes with everything I had, waiting for it all to end. The force of the avalanche dragged me feet first, and I ended up hanging by the arms, with the cascade of white passing over me. And all of a sudden, it stopped. *Fucking hell, I'm still alive!* The ice axes were still driven into the snow. *Shit, I don't want to die like this.*

I reached the ridge with a gargantuan effort and gave the shout we'd agreed on for Séb and Jordi to start to cross. Though it was beyond the steepest wall, the ridge was blanketed in a meter of fresh snow, and we couldn't see even 10 meters ahead. How would we know where to go? It would be tricky to find our way down in the fog. If we took a slight detour to the right, we would return to the highly unstable northeast face, and if we went toward the left, the north face would give us the same treatment. Then it suddenly occurred to me that yesterday I had made it up the ridge to 7,000 meters, and I searched my watch for the GPS stamp of that climb. When Séb arrived, we discussed the situation and agreed we had to follow the route shown on my watch without straying even a little, and hoped to God that it was precise. Jordi emerged from the fog, and as he approached, I saw him look up warily and wave, signaling something I couldn't understand . . .

"Look out!" I heard him cry.

"Fuck! Drive in the ice axes!" I blurted.

An avalanche, fortunately a small one, covered us in snow that came to above our waists. We couldn't even get a break from them on the ridge.

"Shit, shit," said Séb. "We need to get the fuck out of here! We have no control over anything!"

Séb went ahead and began the climb down the ridge. I went a few meters after him, telling him the directions from the watch. Jordi followed me about 50 meters behind, half lost in the fog. We went down as fast as we could, trying hard to cut a path above our knees and dodging the avalanches that slid down the ridge from time to time, camouflaged by the thick fog. Time was arbitrary. One minute it went quickly, the next it was standing still. Jordi had had trouble with the altitude and was getting disoriented. The snow remained highly unstable, triggering minor avalanches. The sound of the effort and breathing, rough and intermittent, was constant, yet at the same time the silence persisted, and we were trapped in a single endless moment. Everything flattened, and some crevasses appeared. Suddenly, we saw the wall of Changtse before us. We were in the North Col! We looked for the ridge, and with a couple of rappels, abseiled down to the bergschrund and the glacier.

When we arrived, I fell flat on the ground, my mind totally empty. Séb and I merged with each other in an embrace and began to laugh and cry. At the same time.

"What in the hell just happened?"

Jordi joined us, and right at that moment, we saw an avalanche sweep the wall we'd been climbing a short time before.

In silence, we set off across the moraine toward the camp. We were 10 kilometers away. As night fell, I wondered how we had gone from euphoria to nightmare in less than a minute. *How many lives have I used up today?* I wondered.

More Than Five Hundred Race Numbers

I hear the alarm on my phone go off just when I've managed to get to sleep. With a clumsy hand, I turn off the thunder that breaks the nocturnal silence, then feel around for the light switch. My eyes are assaulted by the sudden brightness of the hotel room bulb, and I can't open them fully yet. I get up and grab the slice of bread left over from my dinner. I press it to make sure it isn't too stale and spread a thick layer of jam over it with a knife. A mouthful. I close my eyes and feel like order has been restored. It feels so good when the grit beneath your eyelids goes away! A second bite, and a third. The bread becomes a ball in my throat. I can't eat this early. One last mouthful, and I go back to hiding beneath the sheets. I set the alarm to go off again in an hour. I close my eyes and try to sleep. I try to make my mind go blank but don't manage it: thoughts of the upcoming race, provisioning and strategy, seep in through all the cracks in my sleep.

The alarm goes off again. The sheets no longer stick to me;

my eyelids aren't weighed down. I leap out of bed, and the frenetic routine begins: go to the bathroom, drink some water, take off the boxers, and put on the race clothes I laid out the night before, with my number pinned to the back of my shirt. I drink more water and go to the bathroom again. I put on a jacket as a top layer. Now I'm ready. I turn out the light, close the door to the room, and leave the keys under the mat. I jog toward the exit.

When you've repeated this sequence hundreds of times—over five hundred—it loses the charm of a special ceremony and becomes no more than a mechanical, routine way to optimize time. Every once in a while, very sporadically, you get a feeling close to excitement.

Yes, I've accumulated over five hundred race numbers.

The first was pinned on me by my parents before I could walk, for the La Molina New Year's descent. I was two months old, and my father, Eduardo, took me, hanging by the arms, my skis barely grazing the snow. I wasn't yet eighteen months old when my mother pinned another number on me, this time for carrying my own weight during a group hike. I also remember myself at three years old competing for the first time in the cross-country skiing Marxa Pirineu, which includes the 12 kilometers that lead from the Cap del Rec refuge, where I grew up, to the Aransa cross-country station. I managed to complete half the route and finished the last stretch on top of the snowmobile that brought up the rear. From the following year on, I completed the whole race.

Without knowing it, those first forays into sport planted the seed of a lifestyle that has led me to travel all over the world. I've risen in the early hours of the morning over five hundred times to put on a little rectangle with a number stamped on it. Now I'll tell you the story of some of those numbers.

Zegama 2007

The fog was softening a late summer landscape of deep green, fern-filled forests. A delicate layer of microscopic water molecules hung in the air, immobile. If you pass through them quickly, they are refreshing, but they can soak you through in the blink of an eye. A thread of fluorescent orange wool zigzagged between fields of cut grass and marble-white rocks as sharp as knives. My friend and race organizer Alberto and his companions had put the thread there so we wouldn't get lost in the hills of Aratz, before going back into the forest and frightening away the fog demons to find the mud and stone path.

It was Sunday, September 23, and I had a college exam the next day. But at the time, I couldn't have cared less since I was deep in contemplation of the orange tank top up ahead, worn by Raúl García Castán from Segovia. That year, 2007, we had come face-to-face in Andorra, Malaysia, and Japan. Zegama, the most important mountain marathon in the world, takes place in Guipuzkoa. It was the final of the Skyrunner World Series, and if Raúl won, he would take the Skyrunning World Cup. Though the results I'd achieved that season made me feel confident, I knew my opponent performed at his best in long-distance races. For my part, in training, I'd done stretches of 40 kilometers, and even 80, but I hadn't completed the distance of a marathon in an actual race until a week before Zegama, in Sentiero delle Grigne.

During the first half of the route, a group of four of us had run and played nicely together. Apart from Raúl, Jessed Hernández was there, and Tòfol Castanyer from Mallorca too. Jessed was a young talent I'd known for a few years, since when he turned eighteen he'd gone up to live in Estana, a village near where I lived in Montellà. Though he was four years older, we connected immediately, since it was unusual to meet other kids who also liked running in the mountains. That year we had run the Caballos del Viento together, and we'd done 80 kilometers around Cadí and Pedraforca in just over ten hours. Without a doubt, he was one of the most talented runners I'd ever seen. He had a lot of strength. He was pure power. Who knows how far he would have gone if his mind had been more focused on running and training well. His father, Manuel Hernández, and Enric Pujol had formed part of the third expedition to reach the highest point of Broad Peak, at 8,051 meters, in the summer of 1981. When they began to descend, they had an accident and Enric lost consciousness. They had to spend three nights at 7,600 meters, waiting to be rescued. Enric Pujol never woke up.

THE SILENCE WAS ABSURD. ALL I COULD HEAR WAS THE SOUND OF breathing, interrupted by the impact of our steps as we descended at full speed, the crunch of our feet landing on a pile of dry leaves that drew impossible, jumbled shapes in a thick sea of mud. We looked like a group of guys fleeing the enchanted forest in a fairy tale. Suddenly, through the fog, our pursuers caught up with us. They were like two ravenous animals leaping to pounce on their prey, which caused a racket among the dry leaves and branches. It was local runners Zuhaitz Ezpeleta and Fernando Echegaray, who joined us just before we reached the midpoint of the race. Their pace didn't slacken, and they moved ahead of us at a high speed. They were giving it their all, as if they had to end the competition with a sprint. At that moment, I didn't understand why they were doing it. I would soon find out.

Almost at the end of the descent, you go through a tunnel carved out of limestone. It's not very long, but for a few meters in the middle it gets completely dark, and the ground is dotted with rocks of every size that demand your complete concentration. I had never experienced the Zegama race, and YouTube hadn't been invented yet. Despite how much I had heard about what it would be like, the loud murmur that sounded like dozens of distant voices spreading and echoing through the valleys gave me a fright. I was concentrating on treading carefully among the stones, immersed in the darkness, and couldn't allow myself to pay attention to the noise. When we came out into the light at the end of the tunnel, I ran straight into thousands of people equipped with bells and trumpets.

The two Basque runners were raising their arms and cutting a path through the wave of spectators. As they advanced, the racket increased to a level verging on madness. I was so surprised and bewildered that I ran right past the provisioning station. "Cold blood, Kilian, cold blood." I stopped and turned halfway and took a cup of water and a gel, but the excitement and clamor around me made it hard to stay calm. The route went straight ahead toward a steep field of grass and mud. In a race of this distance, I should have taken advantage of the incline to walk a little and pick up the pace before the climb, which was long, eating the gel and drinking some water, but here, that was impossible. With all the shouting, you don't notice the effort you're making. All you can do is run with all your strength because the people push you along with their energy.

Short races, those that take one to four hours to cover between 20 and 40 kilometers, demand a high level of concentration. They aren't anything like the Fully Vertical Kilometer, for example, where one small error can cause you to lose everything and you're in a perpetual bubble, but they can't be compared to a long race, either, during which you have to keep pace and hope the exhaustion won't be too brutal. In these medium-length races, you have to concentrate, that much is true, but even if you make a mistake, you always have enough of a margin to make up for it. You can start running tactically, watch out for the best moment to attack, reserve some moments to rest, or just recover your strength in order to speed up again. I was prepared for these parameters in the Zegama race, until I came out of the tunnel for provisions. From that point on, everything got out of control: the spectators' excitement forced us to pull out all the stops before it was time and to tackle the last 20 kilometers as if we were competing in a high-speed race. It was a nightmare.

After getting past an ascent, during which I overtook the two Basques and opened a gap between myself and my pursuers, I began to hear a murmur even louder than the previous one. I looked up and couldn't believe it: thousands of people were spread over the peak of Aizkorri, occupying every inch. I felt like an unflagging cyclist in the Tour de France, sweating buckets in the middle of July, opening the way toward taking the Tourmalet. The fusion between us, the runners, and the audience was absolute. I have never experienced such a unique feeling in any other part of the world. It's very special.

After getting through the final pass with a strong advantage, I began to notice the guy from Segovia closing in on me, which forced me to run the last 3 kilometers at a bone-crushing pace. Finally, and with great effort, I crossed the finish line in first place, only six seconds before Raúl. Those six seconds—apparently short, but in truth eternal—allowed me to lift the trophy of the Skyrunning World Cup. Those six seconds gave me the ability to begin to live my dream. Those six seconds motivated me to win every competition I've won since then. They were the most valuable six seconds of my career.

This made me think about the fact that winning and losing are separated only by one tiny step, which always depends on minor details.

A few weeks before the Zegama, I had run the Giir di Mont, a 32-kilometer race in the mountains east of Lake Como, in Italy. The prize was a car, a Fiat Panda. (In those days, I was a nineteen-year-old kid who, when he wanted to compete in some faraway race, had to quit paying the electricity bill and live in the dark for a week to be able to cover the registration and the cost of transport.) In that competition, the favorite was the Mexican Ricardo Mejía, who had dominated mountain races for the previous decade: he had won the mythical Sierre-Zinal five times, the Pikes Peak Marathon a few times, and the year before had been champion of the Zegama. It was the second time I had competed against him, and it was barely a week since I'd won my first serious event in Andorra, in the Skyrunning World Cup, where two years earlier I had seen Ricardo for the first time.

That Giir di Mont ended up saving a last surprise for me. I began on the attack, with high momentum, and suddenly found myself ahead of everyone else. Ricardo Mejía followed me with his short but dynamic steps, always running, even on impossible slopes. And he overtook me. From that moment on we took turns, first him ahead and then me. I went ahead of him downhill, and he passed me on the ascents. At the peak of the final ascent, he had a two-minute advantage, and if I wanted to win, I had no choice but to hurl myself down the slope as if my life depended on it. When there was only 1 kilometer left until the finish line, I caught up with him, but I couldn't shake him off. We were 300 meters from the end and stepped onto the tarmac. A slight uphill slope separated us from the finish line, and . . . from the Fiat Panda. Ricardo was way more experienced and smarter than I was, and without leaving me even a second to think about it, he sprinted furiously. He had saved energy during the last descent, and I had emptied my reserves by trying to overtake him. He shot toward the finish line. I watched him move away, unable to do anything. My legs refused to respond to my brain's instructions. *Those* six seconds turned me into a loser.

For a few years, I believed mistakenly that a race was what happened between the starting shot and the finish line. I was blinded by the idea that competition was a binary game between winning and losing, between achieving a good record or a bad one. The need to get the best result prevented me from seeing that the most important thing about Zegama wasn't the encouragement, or the carb-heavy dinner the night before, but the passion of Alberto and Ainhoa, creators and organizers of the race, for turning that village, those mountains, and that day into a magical time for its inhabitants. Or that the real celebration wasn't the one on the podium but the one where everyone gathered around a table to talk—runners, organizers, and spectators alike, all having dinner together in the town's traditional Basque gastronomic club. Or that in Giir di Mont, the competition was less important than the pizzas at Peppa's place afterward. Not being aware of this was the price I had to pay before I could reach the levels of physical fitness and competitive instinct that have given me the knowledge and the mechanics to achieve success.

Hardrock 100

Darkness was falling when we glimpsed the Virginius Pass, rising almost 4,000 meters in the mountains of southern Colorado. Luckily, we had already left the forest, and despite the limited visibility beneath the trees' shadows, the sky was still aglow. A small number of clouds were left, reminding us that a rain- or snowstorm could erupt to cheer up what was left of the day with lightning or hailstones. We were occupying the mountain's territory, and it seemed to want us to know that.

The bright yellow of the rocks was quickly becoming muted, and a ridge towered before us crowned with hundreds of pinnacles whose silhouettes rose against the sky. Between two of those granite towers, in a gap little more than a meter wide, was hidden one of the few passes that cross those mountains directly, without requiring a substantial detour. In that pass, so narrow and inaccessible, was the highest provisions station in the race, and probably one of the highest in any race in the world.

A long tongue of snow showed us the way. The landscape was beginning to split: the snow was white, and everything else—rocks, trees, mountains—was black. We had run over 100 kilometers since that morning, and for the first time my legs were feeling tired. I could no longer make any pointless efforts, like speeding up to get through a more technical stretch or jumping a gate instead of opening it. The way up was tedious, and there was no marked path for us to reach the tongue of snow. We had to climb a slope of loose rock that kept us sliding back down with every step. I tried to move quickly and avoided putting too much weight on the ground in order to trick it. When I finally reached the snow, it was so hard—despite being the middle of July, in daylight, and at over 4,000 meters—that I had to do everything I could to tense my toes and make my sneakers stiff enough to drive in, even if only a few millimeters. I prayed that I wouldn't slip and fall down. Meanwhile, the blue sky faded and became an almost transparent shade of turquoise with a yellow, then orange tint. Finally, it exploded into deep red, before fading into a blue so dark it was almost black, after a brief but intense phase of purple.

I was able to revel in this display of colors just before arriving at the provisioning station. I was with Rickey Gates, an extremely talented runner from the US who could win both 10-kilometer and 50-kilometer races. He is a highly unusual specimen: you're just as likely to find him finishing strong in the Sierre-Zinal race as riding his motorcycle on Route 66, his saddlebags loaded with supplies for a few months' travel from Alaska to Patagonia, or looking for a place to sleep on a farm in Alabama while he crosses the United States from the Atlantic to the Pacific with no assistance. I've known Rickey since my first Sierre-Zinal in 2009. He came in fourth. Since then, we've coincided in many races, from the Alps to Alaska, and he's been my pacer in every competition where I've needed one. Usually, in 100-mile races in the United States, a runner accompanies you on the last 30 or 40 miles to set the pace. Though he can't help you physically, or carry the food and drink, the moral support he offers when you've already run over 60 miles is incalculable. Rickey was my pacer both times I ran the Western States 100, and he also helped me out on the Hardrock 100-Mile Endurance Run, on a long night of relentless rain and lightning.

When the sky was at its reddest, at that moment when it becomes a crimson so intense that it seems almost unreal, we reached the station. Then, I heard a voice:

"Hey, Kilian, want a swig of tequila?"

On that mountain ridge higher than 4,000 meters, in a 2-square-meter space between the rocky walls of two pinnacles flanked by a void on each side, a man dressed in orange and wearing a climbing helmet was filling a metal glass with tequila from a glass bottle. It was Roch Horton, a veteran ultra-distance runner who, after running the race ten times, decided to take charge of this unique provisioning station for the next ten years. As he himself says, "Ten years of receiving and ten of giving."

I still hadn't recovered from my amazement when Rickey exclaimed: "I want one!"

"Okay," I replied, still somewhat disoriented. "One swig won't do me any harm. But just a little, eh? There are still fifty kilometers left, and my legs aren't feeling so fresh anymore."

While Roch poured our tequila and served up a couple of egg, vegetable, and avocado burritos, I noticed there were five other people in that strange place. They had brought a portaledge, a kind of hammock you can use to sleep hanging from a wall.

They had put out cookies, cooked potatoes, sandwiches, burritos, and a poster with the menu of dishes they could prepare up there, even indicating if they were vegetarian or vegan. They also had a couple of portable stoves like those used on expeditions, pots for heating water, and frying pans to satisfy the runners' tastes. We were all sitting on a mattress that, no matter how hard I tried, I couldn't figure out how they had managed to get up there. They'd set it up on a stone wall they had built themselves during the previous weeks.

From that height, we saw how the darkness had spread into the valleys and was now rising and making the colors of the mountains and sky disappear. Meanwhile, Scott Jurek—seven-time winner of the Western States 100, three-time winner of the 246-kilometer Spartathlon, and two-time winner of the Badwater Ultramarathon, who had also triumphed in this race—explained to us how unique this provisioning station was, that it was the only one with a waiting list to volunteer. All the volunteers were Hardrockers, meaning they'd completed this 100-mile race at least once, and all of them had been specially invited by Roch. It's an exclusive privilege to help out at Kroger's Canteen, as the space is known. As much as or more than winning the race.

When I was twenty and participated in a 160-kilometer race, equivalent to 100 miles, what most intrigued me was finding out whether I could cover the distance in one go, and do so at a fast pace. My doubts were dispelled in 2008 in the UTMB, the Ultra-Trail that goes around Mont Blanc. What motivated me about the distance was just knowing if I could compete and win. I faced the challenge of the shortest competition, the Vertical Kilometer, in the same spirit, approaching it with the same training, strategy, and planning. But for longer races, this purely competitive approach and execution was a break from the norm, especially in Europe, where the Ultra-Trail was thought of as a discipline for veterans, to be faced with patience in order to make it to the end in one piece. Indeed, the winner of the last three races had been the Italian runner Marco Olmo. That year he had turned fifty-nine!

After doing longer trainings for a couple of months, I found I could run for eight or nine hours without eating or drinking. This meant I could travel lighter, without having to carry water between the provisioning stations. Studying videos and the partial times of previous winners, I deduced that if I could complete the whole 160 kilometers without walking, I would finish in nineteen hours and my victory would be assured. I prepared well for my long trainings with the minimum equipment necessary, and ran fast for the whole race. I was alone and up ahead by the twentieth kilometer.

That same year of 2008, in the United States, twenty-three-year-old Kyle Skaggs won the Hardrock 100. He was the first to complete it in less than twenty-four hours, and also in a minimalist style, running fast from the first kilometer. Today, with the current preparation and training, the fear of starting out light and fast has dissipated. There is no mystery to it; the difficulty lies in running fast from the first meter to the last. Long-distance running is also a unique and special journey every time. Sometimes it's an inner journey—you experience emotions that intensify with fatigue, and your sensitivity increases; other times, it's external, because you get to know mountains and landscapes deeply from the moment the sun rises until it sets, you accompany the animals as they wake, and they run with you by the light of the moon.

When I compete, I like to be first. I'm the most restless, the most competitive, the most impatient, as you know by now, but at the same time I'm convinced that the satisfaction of victory must be personal and private. I feel a certain aversion to the ostentation of competition. Showing off, taking the stand higher than everyone else, followers and losers, so no one can doubt that we are the best . . . In the end, winning is only internal, individual, inexpressible. It's the same with defeat.

These ceremonies and symbols are what kills competitions. And at the Hardrock 100, they know this perfectly well. By eliminating them, it has become *just* a race, free from paraphernalia and unnecessary displays.

The day after the starting shot, everyone waits in Silverton—also the point of departure—for the last runner to reach the finish line and kiss the stone marking the end of the race. Yes, the stone. You won't find the typical arch with a tape across it here. Instead, there's a rough stone measuring 2 square meters, with the Hardrock 100 logo engraved on it: a mountain ram. After a light snack, the runners, volunteers, and everyone else at the race meet in a school pavilion to celebrate the awesome weekend they've just had. Runners who kiss the stone within forty-eight hours of starting to run, the established limit, receive a certificate. The checkpoint volunteers and pacers are also called together and honored. Everyone plays a role in this competition; everyone is equally important and necessary. Everyone celebrates their love of the sport and of the mountains. That's what a competition should be like.

Ultra-Trail du Mont Blanc

These days, skyrunning is a well-known sport that receives quite a bit of media attention, but ten years ago, only four dudes were practicing it. That all changed in 2006, when Anton Krupicka won the Leadville race in Colorado, one of the most prestigious 100-mile competitions. He was a twenty-something young runner whose surprise win came with a unique aesthetic: minimalist sneakers, short shorts, a bare, tanned chest, and blond locks blowing in the breeze. He also stood for the philosophies of living close to nature and rejecting conflict with others, since according to him, the most important thing was personal exploration. Anton's victory and his message left an even greater mark than the incredible record set a year earlier by the extraordinary Matt Carpenter, who had dominated the Pikes Peak Marathon for nearly two decades.

Two years later, Kyle Skaggs broke the record in the Hardrock, and later that same year, I won the Mont Blanc Ultra-Trail. A fresh new wind was blowing in the sport. The year 2006 also saw the publication of *Born to Run*, a book on the history of Mexican Tarahumara runners, who ran 100 miles shod only in simple sandals. It was the year, too, of the impressive Ann Trason, who killed all the races and beat all the men, and Scott Jurek, who never missed a long-distance race. With the book *Ultramarathon Man*, Dean Karnazes brought trail running to the attention of urbanites and entrepreneurs needing to disconnect and take on a challenge. This series of events, added to the races being organized all over the place, led to an explosive growth of the sport in the next few years. But despite this, men had been running in the mountains for centuries. In fact, there were mountain competitions as far back as 1040, when King Malcolm Canmore organized a hill race in Scotland as a way to select his messengers.

In 2002, when I was starting to run in my first competitions, the star of the moment was Fabio Meraldi, and that was precisely the season when he performed at his highest level. Alongside Bruno Brunod, Matt Carpenter, Ricardo Mejía, and Adriano Greco, he had run the most important peaks in the world in the discipline baptized by Marino Giacometti as *skyrunning* in 1993. I was in awe of these skyrunners, and from my teens I dreamed of competing with them one day. In 2007, I won the Skyrunning World Cup and the Pierra Menta. Then my curiosity was piqued and I wanted to try long distance. In Europe, since being established in 2003, the UTMB has been the race that all runners of this specialty view with a combination of desire and respect.

I didn't realize at the time of my first World Cup win that my life would undergo a radical shift, and not exactly at the level of sport. Overnight, the entire media apparatus made me their central focus, and I lost my anonymity. That was when my love-hate relationship with trail running and everything that surrounds it began. These races are the window where brands and runners put themselves on display. So much media attention often makes you forget the basic elements of the sport: a respect for nature and the community that lives alongside it.

The Fully Vertical Kilometer

The smell of chestnuts doesn't lie: it's the height of autumn. Despite the fact that there are seven hundred runners, there's a convivial atmosphere, typical of a small-town race. Everyone knows everyone. In fact, for many people, Fully (as we call it) has become an excuse for an annual pilgrimage, which some people use to check if working in summer guarantees a good winter performance, and others, to cap off the previous busy months.

The Vertical Kilometer is a race of total sincerity. At this event, it's impossible to pretend. If you're strong, you'll make good time, but if you're weak, there isn't a single technique or tactic that will let you disguise it. This is exactly what makes it an interesting competition that demands intense preparation and great dedication, and also great physical condition on the appointed day.

This race is the touchstone for all mountain athletes, just as the 100 meters is for high-speed runners, or the 10,000 meters for long-distance runners. Everyone knows approximately how long it might take them to climb 1,000 meters, or how many meters they can cover in an hour-long ascent. These are calculation reference points. "If you climb six hundred meters per hour, it will take almost three hours to reach this peak." Reinhold Messner calculated that he climbed 1,000 meters in thirty-five or thirty-six minutes, and since the 1990s, increasingly prepared runners, who follow a specific training regimen, have lowered that time. In this sport, Fully is Mount Olympus. For a couple of decades now, runners of all levels have considered their result in this event to be irrefutable proof of who they are and what they can do. Everyone has done it. From the most exclusive elites, determined to shave off a few impossible seconds, to grandfathers satisfied not to have gotten out of shape with the passing years. And also the youngest, hungriest competitors, eating the minutes year by year.

An hour before the beginning, you start to warm up. You jog without losing sight of the other runners, and you watch them disappear into a landscape shrouded in vineyards. You head for the starting point and leave your jacket in a corner, on the ground. You look up and see two parallel train tracks ahead that converge above, 1,000 meters farther up. When your watch tells you it's not long till the start, you join the line of runners and start getting updated on what's happened in town in the past month. You move forward until the person in front of you leaves you midsentence, because they're already focusing on the starting countdown. When your turn comes, you find yourself alone at the head of the trail, watching the friends you were chatting with a moment ago—about the summer harvest in Valtellina or the result of last weekend's race—start to move away, up the hill. Now it's your turn to break off the conversation with the person behind you. You focus on your countdown. *Go!* You set off quickly but without getting too excited. You try to set your pace. Each step is a victory, and whenever you lift your leg to take another step, you think you're about to throw up. You see 100, 200, 300 meters go by. You don't even realize you've reached 600, 700, 800. You want to touch the 900 mark with your fingers. You want to sprint, but you can't because your legs are brimming with lactic acid. You look up, look down again, and see the white line pass as you fall on the ground. You breathe deeply, your lungs are going to explode, you won't be able to recover at a normal pace, you won't be able to speak until everything is back to normal. You get up, your legs heavy and swollen like jerry cans, to see what time you made, written on a blackboard hanging on the wall. You keep your satisfaction or frustration to yourself.

When you're running against yourself, the winner or loser is always internal. With your joy or disappointment internalized, you calmly set out down the hill with your fellow runners. You imagine the roasted chestnuts waiting for you below. You'll have time to think about everything later on.

Pierra Menta

The smell of Beaufort cheese permeates the corridors of the VTF, a *tout compris* residence with a certain air of decadence, like so many others located at French ski stations. Each year, in the second week in March, its windows turn into a showcase of ski suits in garish colors. On the terrace, a beer provides refreshment from the heat of the sun, which starts to burn brightly after the coldest weeks of winter. In the rooms, water bottles rest empty while the runners, lying in bed, begin to stretch their legs or massage themselves to recover from the effort of this stage of the race. It's ten in the morning on a mid-March day in 2018, and they make the most of the day in their own way, with the satisfaction of having done a day's work. Well, not all of them. Some are still out in the surrounding mountains, trying to beat the time cutoff and catch up to the starting point in the wee hours of the next day. As a friend of mine says, there are three categories in the Pierra Menta: the elite, in pursuit of a place on the podium; the people, fighting for a position on the first page of the result table; and the rabble, who have enough on their hands just finishing each daily stage for the four days this race lasts. This friend has had the good fortune to be a member of all three categories in the Arêches-Beaufort competition in Saboya, for thirty years a competition considered the masterpiece of ski mountaineering.

Some things have to change to progress, while others remain the same and that is exactly their charm, since they transport us to a past when we believed everything was better. With the patina of decadence and tradition, the Pierra Menta has become a mythic sporting event. Here, you willingly accept mistakes you wouldn't put up with anywhere else, since they're part of the uniqueness of the race. That's exactly why it's the best, because it reminds us of a time when ski mountaineering was a difficult, extreme adventure. Like any pilgrimage, it preserves traditions that are enacted year after year. I think of the afternoons at the VTF, the ski suits hung out on the balconies, the chaplain playing the harmonica to thank people for visiting his parish, and the mountains of Beaufortain. Pierra Menta is Daniel waiting discreetly at the end of each stage, hidden behind the fans and journalists, to take our skis and wax them for the next day, asking for nothing in return, just for the personal satisfaction of having had a part in helping us onto the podium. It's going to the little food store in town after the second stage on Thursday, for a stash of cookies to enjoy that afternoon and recover some energy, which always begins to flag after a couple of days. It's seeing the same volunteers every Wednesday when you go to collect your number. It's Pierre-Yves making sure all the runners have an ARVA—the device that emits a signal so you can be found if you get buried by an avalanche—before letting us into the departure pen, after getting up at three in the morning to plot the route by the light of his headlamp. These are the déjà vus that put a complicit smile on our faces because they make us feel part of the Pierra Menta, too.

UNFORTUNATELY, IN THE SPRING OF 2018 I COULDN'T JOIN MY FELLOW runners to eat polenta on Sunday afternoon in the Arêches-Beaufort hall. I was lying down in a clinic, 300 meters away, while a doctor showed me some x-rays.

"You can see the fracture to the fibula very clearly. When the inflammation in your ankle goes down, you'll have to do an MRI to make sure you don't have any torn ligaments. You know, in cases like this, that's where the problems usually are."

Who would have thought it the night before, when I had already pictured myself celebrating my victory. I was not disappointed, no. Now I knew that it was just a bone fracture, which doesn't usually bring any complications. I was convinced that even if I had to cancel an expedition and my races at the beginning of the season, I would be training and climbing mountains again in no time at all. Mostly, I was sad for my fellow runner, Jakob Hermann, who had been running the race for the first time but wasn't able to win because of my fall.

It had been a fantastic last day, with tricky conditions. The organizers, showing off their home brand, had not taken the easy route and had planned trails that made the race harder, with more downhill stretches on un-skiable snow. The rapport I'd established with Jakob, my teammate, was perfect, though this was only the second race we had done together. Before we started the final stage we were in the lead, with an advantage of just over three minutes, but we were feeling increasingly strong since we could tell that our rivals were losing stamina. That morning we had set out calmly, but since we saw we had time to spare on the uphill stretches, we'd gone hard so we wouldn't have to take any risks on the way back down. Almost by accident, we'd gained that three-minute advantage over our pursuers on the last uphill slope. It was snowing hard, but this didn't prevent the thousands of spectators—who make the annual pilgrimage to this event to cheer us on—from stoically tolerating it. We waved, causing the decibel level of the cries and applause to double.

We began our descent with wide turns, moving neither too fast nor too slow. On one of those turns, I felt my ski get embedded under the snow. It was stuck, and my body began to fall to one side. I got up to continue downhill, but—*ouch*. When I put my weight back on my leg, it hurt like hell. I got down as best I could, hardly putting any weight on my left side, and when I reached the transition, Jakob was waiting for me, ready to go up again. While he helped me put my skins on, I told him I'd hurt myself—I didn't know how seriously, but something wasn't quite right. As I started upward, the pain flooded my entire leg. *Is it my knee? A bone? The ligaments?* I tried to take steps without suffering, and for a moment it seemed like the pain eased with the warmth of the effort, but after a couple hundred meters of slope, a stretch began with some bends and I noticed that when I turned my leg, I couldn't rest it back on the ground. I heard a click-click with every step, feeling like each time I put my weight on it, something twisted inside me. Jakob wanted to help me, but there was nothing to be done.

"Do you want us to quit?"

"No," I answer. "Let's keep going. I think it'll be okay once it warms up. It's only two or three hundred meters to the top."

I went on a little more. The others still hadn't caught up with us, but they were getting closer. With every step, I let out a cry of pain, though I tried to stifle it. I pressed forward a few more meters, but then I was certain I couldn't go on. My leg couldn't support my weight, and I was dizzy with pain. We were a few meters away from achieving our dream, but an astronomical distance from touching it with our fingers. I moved myself to the side of the trail and watched the runners go by, each on their way to their own personal victory.

I CAME TO COMPETE IN THE FOUR-DAY RACE AT PIERRA MENTA FOR the first time in 2007, when I was only twenty. It was also the first time I was in the adult category in an event, and I was strong but didn't have much self-control. I had started out with a fourth-place position in the first Skyrunning World Cup event, but I'd set the pace for the more experienced runners, who passed me on the last downhill stretch. In my second race as a senior, the World Cup in the Valais in Switzerland, I caused a big surprise when I overtook the local runner Florent Troillet on the last ascent and wore a victory crown, beating two of my rivals, Florent Perrier and Guido Giacomelli. After the race, Florent Troillet came to see me and asked if I had a team for the Pierra Menta. I didn't catch the hint and said I would love to go, that maybe I'd find someone from the French or Spanish team who wanted to do it. Florent is shy and not a big talker, a quality I've always appreciated, and maybe that's why we made such a great team over the next few years. He didn't say anything, and there was the kind of awkward silence that happens when you're waiting for someone to speak and instead they look you straight in the eye. It took him a minute to ask if I wanted to go with him. I jumped for joy inside: one of the best ski mountaineers of the moment wanted to compete with me in the most important race in the world!

For the third race that year, I arrived in Arêches-Beaufort in heavy snow, and Florent and I went out skiing right away to stretch our legs. After an hour, he sounded me out:

"What do you say we do some accelerations?"

What was I supposed to say? *Let's go!* I followed him for four or five accelerations, and then we went down to the room we'd be sharing for the next few days. In the morning, the sun came out and continued to shine for all four days of the competition.

We barely spoke, even during the stages, when every once in a while we'd say something like "*On y va tranquille et on accélère doucement*" ("We go slowly and gently accelerate") as we attacked an uphill slope, and not much else. We didn't speak much during the long afternoons in our room, either. We told the occasional story, something interesting about our training, or very occasionally shared a thought to break the silence. . . . Sometimes you don't need to speak to someone to feel at ease.

From the first day, each of us knew what the other wanted without them having to ask. If one of us needed to slow down or wanted to quicken the pace, or if one of us needed a drink or a gel. If one of us needed to help or be helped, or if we wanted to speak or be quiet. It's true what the most seasoned athletes say: in a ski-mountaineering race, you begin as friends but cross the finish line as brothers. This was definitely the case for us.

Without any excitement, without wanting to believe it, we won the first stage; the next day, the second; and on the third day, again. When we set out on the fourth day, we weren't so sure. It's such a long race that no matter how much of an advantage you have, by the end, anything can happen. Luckily, though, nothing happened this time, and when we finally saw the arch, we couldn't believe it. At that moment, I felt so *happy*. It's a feeling that can manifest in many ways. It's a tingling that rises gradually up your legs until it reaches your heart and explodes in a burst of adrenaline. You could break your shinbone and you wouldn't notice the pain. Even if you attacked a stone wall with your fists. It leaps from your heart into your head and surges all through your body. When this happiness comes in a team race, it's really special. Your ego is bursting, but your adrenaline is diluted into a kind of love because you've shared some important moments, and most of all, you've helped make someone else happy. This was the beginning of some sweet years. Florent and I made a fearsome team, and individually, I began to eat everything up, both in skiing and in running.

The year before that Pierra Menta, I experienced the profound feelings of competition for the first time, when I gave up the junior category to compete in the adult category in the European Cup final, and realized, from that unexpected victory, that I could go far and win serious races. I felt them again in Valerette, Switzerland, and then in the first Pierra Menta, my first time competing in the Skyrunning World Cup, the Zegama when I had just left my teens behind, and a few more races over the next few years.

Yet despite all this, my excitement when I crossed a finish line began to dwindle, and I no longer felt such a rush of adrenaline. I didn't feel drunk on happiness, and I was increasingly content just to be satisfied. Satisfaction can often be enough, but when the intense feelings of winning have become routine, happiness begins to seem flat and mundane. It isn't sufficient. Calvin and Hobbes captured it well in a strip: "Happiness isn't good enough for me! I demand euphoria."

Once, after seeking this lost feeling, I realized it was better to let it be and abandon the search. Now I think that reminiscing about our well-being in the past can obscure the possibilities of the present. As always, a good memory leaves a nice aftertaste, and our brain will try to bury anything that gets in its way. You don't need to maintain this excitement to pull out all the stops in a race, especially if you know that when you arrive, even after fighting tooth and nail in a world-class competition, at most you'll have the satisfaction of confirming that you're still in shape. This is more than enough to give it your all.

When you have this revelation, it lifts a great weight off your shoulders, because it means while you're not euphoric, you also won't be disappointed. I remember so well the tears in Baqueira-Beret in that first World Cup, when I broke my boot when I was in the lead on the final descent, and I didn't make it onto the podium. And how I thought I could never show my face again when I was in the lead in a world championship with an advantage of over two minutes, and my bindings broke on the first turn of the descent. I was so angry, damn it, and I spent a week cursing my luck. Now it's sweet to remember those frustrations.

WHAT REALLY DRIVES ME TO MAKE THE PILGRIMAGE TO PIERRA MENTA year after year isn't the emotional reward for my ego but the immediate satisfaction, the smell of the Beaufort cheese, the sunny afternoons on the VTF terrace. Going up to the wild and jagged ridge of the Grand Mont, and hearing the murmur as people approach.

What we're really seeking and what keeps us coming back is a combination of all these little things, and more. Victory is the cherry on the cake. But we mustn't forget that what really matters is for the batter to be moist and the jam to be of high quality, since in the end there's only one cherry, and when the cake is sliced, only one person gets it. As the years go by, not even the winner remembers its flavor, but everyone can recall the sweet aftertaste of the jam.

Sierre-Zinal

The sun is about to rise, and in the cold and drowsy dawn air, you can hear the murmur of quick footsteps and sleepy voices. One of those footsteps is mine. Just like every year, I've had to get myself up in time so as not to miss the bus. Dressed in race clothes with a jacket on top, I look for an empty seat. I sit down toward the back, and almost that instant the bus starts to move. You can't hear a sigh, but the jostling of the bus from navigating the switchbacks between pinnacles prevents us from taking a nap. Despite the driver's skill, it takes fifty minutes to go the 24 kilometers that separate the town of Zinal, at the end of the glacier where the valleys die, from Sierre, the city on the plain of Valais, where vineyards, industry, medieval castles, and the noise of the highway contrast with green countryside dotted with tiny villages, and silence punctuated only by rivers rushing down from the high, snowy peaks. I took this bus for the first time ten years ago. It was nerve-racking! I was so excited and terrified of failure that I hadn't slept all night. It's interesting to see how sport has changed my personality since then. Before becoming the calm person I am today who coolheadedly tackles his major goals, I was a bundle of nerves who always spent race days completely worked up.

When I was seventeen, the European ski-mountaineering championships took place in Andorra. Since it was near where I lived, and to my surprise I had been a youth world champion the previous year, I wanted to give it a shot, and I knew everyone wanted me to. I had prepared painstakingly and trained like never before. One day I had even left Montellà with my skis on my back, gone through La Llosa river valley by bike, and from there, walking and skiing, I hopped over to Andorra through the Montmalús to reach Canillo and train a couple of times on the vertical route before going home.

The day of the race arrived, and without having slept a wink, I went to the start along with the rest of the team, with an hour to spare. After a quick-paced warm-up, I was ready to start. In that vertical race the runners left one by one, so later it was impossible to know if I was going fast enough. There was no strategy I could use to tell, so I had to give it my all from the start to the finish. The line at the start was getting shorter. Though I'd already taken my headphones off and wasn't listening to any of the ten songs I'd chosen for motivation, I was oblivious to everything going on around me. All I could make out was the beep-beep-beep that announced, minute by minute, the beginning of the route for the other youth athletes ahead of me. My heart was beating faster and faster and leapt into my mouth with every beep. When the runner in front of me set out at high speed and I was left alone at the red line sprayed in the snow, I felt like my heart had stopped. The pace of my heartbeat gradually slowed, but with every pulse I felt like a bomb was exploding right in front of me. I don't know what the referee said to me; I didn't understand. Beep! I looked ahead for the first time, trying to calculate the speed of my competitors. Beep! It was cold, but my hands were sweating, and with every heartbeat my body shook. Beep! The starting signal went off, and I felt like my legs had lost all of their strength. I was afraid I was going to collapse right there. But no. My limbs responded unconsciously. I felt my muscles activate and contract as they always had. I set out fast. Really fast. Too fast. I sprinted 1,000 meters, giving it my all, but the race had a 1,000-meter slope, and I soon began to pay the price for the stupidity of that unnecessary effort. Luckily, in the end I was able to recover a little and repair the mistakes of my excess effort at the beginning, influenced more by my nerves than my brain, that came close to making me lose the race.

NOW, ON THE BUS, I'M HAVING TROUBLE STAYING AWAKE. THOUGH I still feel a desire to compete, there's no trace of the nerves and tension of years ago. To wake myself up a bit, I start thinking about the race and go over the route, which I know well after participating eight times.

If I had to describe the mountain race I would least like to run, I'm sure I would say that it's short, without many downhill slopes or long stretches of trail, or that it has a wide dirt road and many kilometers of flat terrain. It would have no rocks on the trail or technical terrain, and would pass by peaks that call out to you to climb them but really are just there for decoration, since you have to run through their foothills without coming close to the highest parts. If any race fits these parameters, it's Sierre-Zinal. And despite this, I'm crazy about it.

I guess what excites me about this race is exactly that. It's run in terrain where I don't feel comfortable, where I know I have to face my weak spots as a runner and fight those weaknesses in order to win. For me, that's what gives competition meaning—seeking difficulty and embracing it. And the fact that the route is the opposite of what I prefer is exactly why I approach it as a challenge with all the necessary ingredients to keep me interested. Its organization is perfect, sublime, and it has a long history. The greatest specialists in the world get together each year, making up an odd mixture of mountain and road runners, skyrunners and orienteers, on terrain that is favorable to some and not to others. Too flat for those of us who are happy on the highest ridges. Too steep for those who run marathons in under two hours ten minutes. Too long for the mountain runners and orienteers. Too short for the long-distance runners. You can already see that with such a variety of styles among the participants, this is the perfect setting for a spectacle and a fight, undesirable elements for all of us. That's why there's every reason for us to put on our numbers.

AT THE STARTING POINT, THERE'S A MIXTURE OF NERVES AND JOYOUS excitement. Some people smile, and others are anxious to try to get a few centimeters ahead, positioning themselves close to the first line. I don't like to put myself ahead, and I only go to the first row if I predict complications at the start, if the terrain narrows early, or if I think I might fall easily. Generally, I prefer to be in the second or third row. People start too fast and they often push you, or in ski mountaineering, someone might break your pole by accident or take the skin off one of your skis. Furthermore, in the first row, the runners' anxiety is more intense. It seems like the activity is more important than it really is, and there's always some journalist who wants you to grin and pose or say something stupid.

The horn blows, and the stampede begins. I pass from the third to the sixth or seventh row; everyone gets ahead, sprinting and elbowing me out of the way. I open my arms a little and make space for myself so I don't lose my balance, then take a run up and find my pace. After 100 meters, most of the fifty or so runners I had in front of me have drastically slowed their pace. I pass them on one side of the road and catch up with the group in the lead.

We've covered just over a kilometer, and we make for a steep dirt trail. A dozen runners who know each other from other races end up alone together. There're a couple of Kenyans, two Colombians, Petro Mamu from Uganda, Robbie Simpson from Scotland, and the odd European or American. Halfway up the steep ascent, Petro, who won the IAAF mountain running world championship just two weeks earlier, begins to speed up in short, intense bursts to break up the group. After a couple of attacks, we let him go. *There's a lot of race left, and these efforts so early could cost me later on*, I think. One of the Kenyans, Geoffrey Ndungu, the mountain race specialist who has run marathons in two hours eight minutes, and William Rodríguez, a Colombian who's always at Sierre-Zinal, follow him. Behind him, we're trying as hard as we can, our calf muscles accumulating lactic acid, and our lungs fighting for more space inside our chests. The leading trio is just over a minute away, and they don't gain any more time.

When we reach the high point of the climb, a long forested stretch begins. This is where my tired mountain runner's legs usually make me feel like a snail surrounded by road-running gazelles, but to my surprise, we move ahead quickly together until we reach the first three runners at the race's midpoint, right at the entrance to Chandolin. We leave the town and about 10 kilometers of flat terrain behind, along paths and trails that lead us to the highest point in the race, the Hotel Weisshorn, at almost 2,500 meters. This is where my legs remind me that on terrain like this, I'm not a fast runner but more like a tractor, and I can't prevent the runners who are more used to the road from starting to lunge through the air as if in flight. I pay no attention to the wise little voice in my head that tells me to slow my pace and stay in my comfort zone, and I keep fighting the heaviness of my legs, trying to lengthen each step a little more, trying to push my feet forward faster. I struggle for one or two minutes, knowing that after the hotel comes a stretch more favorable to my condition, and on the small uphill slope just before the highest point of the race, I pass William and Petro, who seem to be paying for the effort they made at the start.

I run by the front of the Hotel Weisshorn and have three runners ahead of me at a one-minute interval. There's no time to look up, but I glimpse the silhouettes of the surrounding mountains out of the corner of my eye. It's an idyllic landscape, a typical Swiss postcard scene with log cabins in bright green fields, cows grazing here and there. I recognize the sharp ridge joining the peaks of Zinalrothorn and Ober Gabelhorn, and the perfect pyramid of Matterhorn outlined behind them. To the west, the imposing north face of the Weisshorn (which gives the hotel its name) dazzles the valley, and to the right, the Dent Blanche casts its shadow. I try not to lose focus remembering the good times I've spent on those peaks. *That's what I really love. What the hell am I doing suffering here, trying to overtake that gang of gazelles?* But my legs know the answer. I keep running, trying to speed up and gain time with every step. Deep down, I know I love the stupid, simple game of competition. I focus again, because now the more favorable stretch is coming up, the descent, where my mountain runner's technique gives me an advantage over the others.

Little by little, the gaps shorten, and I pass Geoffrey Ndungu and then José David Cardona from Colombia, and finally, 3 kilometers from the finish line, I pass Robbie Simpson, one of the most talented and accomplished young runners, as much on the road as in the mountains.

What comes next feels familiar: without resting, but feeling secure, I run the rest of the way until I reach the end.

WE'VE FINISHED. I'VE RECOVERED MY BREATH AND WE'VE HAD OUR pictures taken. I go to the anti-doping test station, stopping to pose for selfies and sign some autographs on my way.

"Congratulations! You're amazing!" I hear someone say.

It's a woman of about forty. Since she's sweating and dressed in shorts, I ask how the race went for her.

"Good. Well, it was really tough. It took me five hours, twice as long as you, but I'm a teacher and I can't train that much. I just go out on weekends and some weekday afternoons."

I congratulate her sincerely and keep going toward the test station. After a few meters, someone else crosses my path.

"Good work, dude!" says a guy who must be about my age, a happy belly showing under his shirt. "It was too long for me. I'd never done sports in my life, and last year while we were building a chalet up here, a coworker and I saw the race and I made a bet to run it. But after twenty kilometers I couldn't go on and ended up walking. But you . . . you're an alien, dude!"

I finally make it to the building where the anti-doping test station is, and as I collapse into a chair with the bottle of water I need to drink to extract the ninety milliliters needed for the test from my dehydrated body, I start thinking about my brief conversations on the way here. Those people were anonymous and, in a certain sense, slow runners.

For me, running is easy, and doing it fast is, too. Winning, on the other hand, is harder and demands many hours of training and effort. But without wanting to seem arrogant, winning has also become relatively easy for me over the years. In the end, I do virtually nothing else all day, and I hardly think about anything else, either. I run and make money. Today I've earned a few thousand euros, and thanks to my victories, brands want to sponsor me. That teacher and the guy who works in construction, on the other hand, will never be on the news or sign an autograph. In the end, it's paradoxical, since the world would work just as well without runners, but without anyone to teach us to write and count, or build the houses we live in, life would truly be difficult.

I feel bad about myself. Today I've earned money from a useless activity. I've monopolized the attention and admiration of children and adults, and all I've done is put one foot in front of the other faster than them. I accept that, inwardly, running is everything to me. On the other hand, outwardly I've come to terms with the fact that it's pointless.

Come on, Kilian, don't be so simplistic.

I don't believe that sport has no social function. Since the Roman period, it has served as entertainment, and with the rise of wellness in modern times, it has promoted a healthy lifestyle, diet, and exercise, and set standards that show the rewards of hard work and discipline. But today, despite everything, sport seems to be going back to its roots, to spectacle and to the Roman circus. In the modern version, there are millions of spectators in front of a screen, watching a small number of athletes perform their acrobatics, while they celebrate by drinking beer and eating junk food.

Competitive sport is also overvalued, and increasingly exposes the dark side of human nature. The monetization and mythification of sports have turned it into a classic spectacle, causing it to be simplified, and the results to be organized more hierarchically. In the Olympic model, what matters is your place on the podium, with the winner situated visually above those who come second and third, and all three obscure the existence of the other athletes. People only remember the results and the winners. At the same time, countries exploit their athletes' success to reinforce nationalist discourse, even those countries that are in decline. Just as in climbing victory is signaled by planting a flag on a mountain's summit, in world championships or in the Olympic Games, national symbols become propaganda tools.

For our part, athletes have come to believe that winning makes us better than the person in second place, since everyone applauds and congratulates us. This has allowed us to sign contracts and experience the illusion of relative fame. But in this context, sport loses its essence and enters a different realm, obsessed with winning at all costs. Of course, everyone has their own technique, but it's clear enough that the temptation to cheat is high. There's always someone who breaks the rules of the game to increase their chance of victory, which, by definition, is futile.

Luckily, the sports I practice still preserve a solid amateur component. They've been spared the black mark of the period of doping by big teams or countries, when publicity and reputation were considered much more important than athletic performance.

Although in mountain climbing, victory was glorified more and practitioners often resorted to drugs like amphetamines and corticosteroids or to using oxygen, trail running and ski mountaineering were marginal, minority sports and had no influence beyond a few media channels with limited reach. Somehow this was what saved them. In the first decade of this century there's been a certain amount of change with the boom in mountain races, Ultra-Trails, and to a lesser degree ski mountaineering. Social networks have begun to dictate what sparks interest more than traditional media, and minority sports have carved out a space for themselves. Trail running has achieved this to a strong degree. With this evolution, the mythification of champions, the false sense of victory, and the power of winners have taken hold, and some competitors have begun to cheat.

A few months after Petro Mamu competed in the Sierre-Zinal, the athletic federation handed him a sixth-month suspension for taking a prohibited medication during the world championships, which took place two weeks before the Swiss race. When someone gets caught doping, I don't get mad because I think I should have won. What really bothers me is that their performance isn't authentic and isn't a valid reference point, and it sets a bad example for sport in general.

That's why we have be tough and support the fight against doping. Not everything goes, and the most important thing is to know our limits. But maybe the best weapon against doping and cheating is to de-mythify the sport and get rid of the podium. There's no such thing as a hero.

NOT EVERYTHING IS BLACK-AND-WHITE. WHILE IT'S TRUE THAT THE Olympic approach and the current system have distorted the values of competition, they've also helped many to progress. People have invested a lot of money, and not only have first-class competitors appeared but also major progress has been made in the study of biomechanics and outstanding training methods have been devised. Climbing walls have become a basic tool for getting the most out of climbing techniques. Technical sprinting circuits have allowed us to train for the transition of putting skins on and taking them off in ski mountaineering. Vertical races on prepared ski slopes have provided a better method for improving physique and resistance, which would have been impossible in the mountains, where the required technique prevents an athlete's full physical potential from being deployed. But while they are interesting in terms of performance and necessary for progress, these tests should not be confused with the ultimate nature of the sport. If, one day, when someone says "ski mountaineering" the first thing that comes to mind is a three-minute race on an indoor circuit, or when someone mentions "trail running" we picture someone running in circles around a large city with artificial obstacles, that will mean we're in terrible shape and we've taken a wrong turn.

IT SHOULD BE CLEAR THAT, FOR ME, THIS IS AN EASY POSITION TO take. Or for us, the majority of Westerners. It's clear that we have the good luck to practice a sport just for pleasure, and those who compete do it largely to feed their egos. In many parts of the world, though, sport isn't the final goal but rather a way to make a living. In countries where life isn't easy, competition becomes a route to survival. The goal of fame, if it arrives one day, isn't to satisfy an athlete's vanity but to buy a farm for their family to work. But let's not kid ourselves: victory is so tantalizing, and money is so appealing, that in any part of the world people can lose sight of why they run.

I DON'T MIND ADMITTING THAT I MAKE QUITE A BIT OF MONEY COM-peting, but I also spend a ton to be able to do so. I was born in Europe, I've had the good luck to do this for pleasure, and I've never had to see it as a way to make a living, though I'd be lying if I claimed that was never an incentive, especially when I remember that at the beginning of my career I was pretty broke. But I knew deep down that if it didn't work out I could earn a living somehow or another, or keep studying and take whatever path interested me most. I live in the first world, after all.

This is why I've always considered myself an *amateur*. The word is a Gallicism that comes from the Latin *amator*, meaning "one who loves." And there's no doubt that I'm in love with the sports I practice. If today I'm a professional, professionalism for me isn't only about competing and getting good results but also about doing events, movies, and photo shoots, giving talks, and helping design equipment and teams with sports brands.

I'VE ALWAYS WONDERED WHAT I WOULD'VE DONE IF I HADN'T CHOSEN sport as a way of life. The truth is that I have no idea. I guess competition has played an important role in my life for different reasons.

I grew up in a sparsely populated rural area and began my education at a school where the parents and teachers were hippies. I went to high school in a small city, though it was large enough for social stereotypes to be more pronounced and differences less accepted. Until then I didn't know that I was a shy, introverted child who understood little of other children and who was, in turn, little understood by them. I learned the contrast between what was considered normal and what was seen as abnormal. I belonged to the second group. The only concern I showed to anyone was my passion for mountain sports. That's why the song the other kids greeted me with when I passed them spread like wildfire all around me: "Tra-la-la, jumping over the mountains, skipping across the valleys, here comes Kilian, la-la-la-laaaa." The tune was from a TV show that was apparently popular at the time.

I guess I began to compete because of a need for recognition and to find myself during my teens. I had to try to put myself on the map, to know who I was, so others would know me, too. Since I never liked to lose, even as a child, my shyness presented no obstacle and was in fact an advantage for fighting backbreakingly hard, if necessary. That was my way of saying, "Here I am! This is me!"

In the early years, my wins took me by surprise and brought me fulfillment because no one expected anything from me, and I had fun trying to compete in this or that race. Almost before I'd realized, I started getting invited to events, and people asked me to progress. It wasn't a game anymore. Though my mother—who went everywhere with me—and my trainers were all happy to see me win, luckily they did not attach much importance to the results and didn't have any expectations. I believe their attitude saved me.

Once I was out of my teens, my need for recognition vanished. I could have stopped competing because I could tell I had an aversion to the podiums, the hierarchy the results imposed, the mythification . . . but when it's fairly easy for you to win, it's hard to stop. In all honesty, every victory feeds your euphoria, you feel strong, and you feel loved. If you could choose euphoria, would you be content with just happiness?

In the end, when I come down from the crest of this wave of feelings, I can see clearly what competition really gives me: it always challenges me, making me doubt my abilities and ask myself what shape I'm in at the time. I never know if I'm training hard enough or slacking off, and when I want to be the best version of myself, I look for and analyze every small detail, to progress and explore my limits. And when I have other famous competitors to contend with, it's easier to motivate myself to train hard. What really drives me is to try to win races in which the uncertainty of the result is as high as possible.

Yes, I like winning—there's no doubt about it—but I also

like losing. I like spending time with new runners who are more motivated than me, better trained, and have a stronger desire to reach the top. Competing by their side recharges my batteries, motivates me to learn from and battle it out with them, if I can. Then the competition becomes, in part, a checklist I use to test whether I'm capable of keeping up the level I demand of myself, and whether my training or the changes I introduce get the results I'm hoping for. Apart from all that, does anyone know a better high-intensity training than participating in a world championship, or competing in the UTMB or the Sierre-Zinal?

EVEREST IN
FALL

As the rains arrive in Europe, and the days get shorter and become shrouded in gray, in the Himalayas, the clouds bid the peaks farewell with bated breath, and the sun settles in to stay. Fall is a beautiful season in Nepal. With just a small backpack with the four basic things you need, you can run from valley to valley, eat and sleep in the villages, and climb mountains every day.

We left Tibet in early September, and I spent the fall of 2016 at home. After running a couple of races to ask my body if it was still working after a monthlong expedition, the fall embraced me. These are the gray months in the north, a period when people shut themselves inside to wait. Outside, it rains and snows. The darkness lengthens, but the nights seem short when you go out to climb mountains. For me, this is the time when the year begins and ends, when I think about and analyze the season. What do I do? Train, train, train. The simple, difficult work routine that gets disrupted during the rest of the year, when I'm always going from race to race or from mountain to mountain.

Every time I finish an activity, people have varied reactions. There is incomprehension and rejection, because some people either can't understand what I do or associate it with dishonesty, doping, and cheating. There are also those who react with admiration. Although not everyone can completely understand what I do, people are impressed by names like Everest and by the numbers—something everyone can comprehend and compare, even if they don't know with what. There are also those who are indifferent—maybe they're the smartest ones—plus, finally, a small minority who do understand and who come up with the nerdiest theories to motivate themselves or approach their own projects with a new perspective. After all, the world is a varied place.

Reintegrating into society after some time away isn't easy. In my case, I have to go back to being Kilian Jornet—not the person, but the name, the figure. The life in which people recognize me freaks me out and makes me panic in a way that's difficult to describe. The most antisocial part of me was very comfortable in the Himalayas, and I didn't feel like going back to a life of community obligation.

When these ideas started worrying me as we were taking our tents down and packing up our equipment to leave base camp, I had an idea:

"Hey, Séb, listen. What do you say we send a message announcing my death? It would spread like wildfire on Twitter and become the truth. Then we'll tell Emelie, my parents, and my sister it was a lie, that I just said it so I could get my freedom and anonymity back."

Though it seemed like a great idea to me, Séb didn't share my enthusiasm.

"Maybe you don't need to be such a jerk, man. Have you thought of the fact that you'd hurt a lot of people's feelings by accident?"

"To hell with people!" I blurted immediately. I pondered it a little and, after a while, ended the conversation, but I wasn't completely convinced. "Well, okay, I agree, maybe this isn't the time . . ."

With my head down, I went on picking up the last things scattered around the campsite, mentally preparing myself for the fact that I would soon have to be surrounded by swarms of people. Yes, you're right: I'm going to be an unbearable old man. If I'm already like this at thirty, within a few years I'll be one of those grandpas who open the curtain a crack to peer out suspiciously when a stranger walks by their window, or waits quietly inside when a friend knocks on the door, hoping the friend will think they're not at home. Yikes, what a frightening thought. No one will be able to stand me!

JUST AS WHEN I FINISH A RACE I NEED A WHILE TO RECOVER, I NEED A while to digest and let things settle. But people, and the media, are impatient. They want to know right away what you experienced and how it felt. The truth is that I don't like it when they come over to ask me questions, and sometimes all I can say is some bullshit that's supposed to be funny, or something automatic and trivial, completely lacking in interest, which can even end up seeming disdainful. I feel as if they're sticking their fingers down my throat to make me throw it all up before I've had time to digest it.

What I love most about going on expeditions is that I can

disconnect from the world, from everything and everyone. I can just bond with the people I love and the mountains, with no eyes watching and analyzing my every word and movement. That's why, when I reenter the *real world*, I need time to reacclimate.

I had another brilliant idea: I told Emelie and my agent that I wanted to disappear. Though they didn't feign surprise when I mentioned it, they accepted it skeptically and told me my role was to motivate others to practice sports and get to know nature . . . In other words, let's just leave it there.

I didn't choose to be admired. In fact, there are moments when it disgusts me. I've never wanted to be a role model to anyone. I'm sorry, it's just not something I chose. And at the same time, I don't ever want to have to do or stop doing anything for anyone.

THE LEAVES DRIFTED FROM THE BRANCHES TO THE GROUND, AND THE snow took its brush to the mountains. Little by little, I grew used to people again, and, hiding out in Norway, I recovered my dreams of the mountains. These are the dreams only you yourself can understand, since in them you aren't looking for difficulty, great heights, or beauty, but rather you're searching for yourself. Each mountain is the shape of the person who wants to climb it; a solitary ascent isn't the one you feel with your hands on the rock but the one that beats inside you, while on the outside your body is fighting. Far from the noise, where a mountain is just a geographic feature, you live a whole life because every mountain climbed, every friend lost, and every aborted ascent leaves you with a scar etched on your skin.

Maybe that's what old age is: a body with no room left for

any more scars. Is that when I'll be able to climb mountains with the true freedom of maturity? When I've understood that to love is to give up my freedom, and that freedom is the acceptance of unconditional love? By then, my body won't be able to follow the pace set by my mind, and my scars will long for a younger body. I want to be an eighty-year-old boy who senses the urgency of the moment without needing to create a future. I want to experience every phase of my love for the mountains with total madness, with my eyes shining brightly, my heart beating wildly and out of control, my legs shaking from having just climbed up a mountain. Until, when I'm truly old, my body stops working for good.

Partners in Dreams

It was the summer of 1938. Anderl Heckmair, Fritz Kasparek, Ludwig Vörg, and Heinrich Harrer reached the summit of the Eiger, in the Swiss Oberland, after completing the first climb of the north face in history. This meant that the last challenge in the Alps had been overcome, just as Heckmair would write in his book *Die drei letzten Probleme der Alpen* (*The Last Three Problems of the Alps*). The other two had been cracked during that same decade, and like the Eiger, they also came in the form of ice and rock: these were the north faces of Matterhorn and the Grandes Jorasses. The first was conquered by brothers Franz and Toni Schmid in 1931, and the second by Martin Meier and Rudolf Peters three years later. The pioneer who ascended the three north faces was the great French guide and mountaineer Gaston Rébuffat, between 1945 and 1952. Later, they would be climbed in winter, solo, and at high speed—all three in just a few hours.

These days, climbing those walls is no great achievement, and they've been tackled with a whole range of combinations. But those cold rock faces of uncertain quality still inspire the

dreams of thousands of mountaineers, year after year. Sometimes I wonder what drives these fantasies, and I've concluded
that when you move through this terrain, imagining yourself
at the top of the Eiger, you feel the attraction of not only the
immense black wall but also all its history, the memory and
fascination of everything you've read or heard. You're not just
conquering walls of rock and ice; inside, you're accompanied
by Heckmair's experience, too. You see Reinhold Messner and
Peter Habeler climbing in just ten hours, revolutionizing mountaineering and the Alps. And you remember many more feats
that you've dreamed of since you were a child. You don't really
know if you climb mountains because of their beauty, or if
they are extraordinary for what they represent, always filtered
through what you've read or been told.

In the liturgy of mountaineering, few walls have been
praised as much as those three in the Alps, conquered in the
1930s. Even though I had already imagined climbing them when
I was a boy, I had never decided to write in a notebook what it
meant to fulfill this dream. Until one day by sheer coincidence I
ran into Simón on Mont Blanc.

Simón

Chamonix is the only city in the world where you can walk
down the street calmly in ski boots and Gore-Tex in the middle
of August when it's thirty degrees Celsius without feeling like an
eccentric. It's even occurred to me that there must be people who
go to work at the office in jeans and a T-shirt, then put on their
mountain boots after dinner, wrap a coil of rope around their
shoulder, and go out for a few beers at the bar.

The first thing you see on arrival when you approach by road is a sign saying CHAMONIX MONT BLANC, with a second line below, LA CAPITALE MONDIALE DE L'ALPINISME (THE WORLD CAPITAL OF MOUNTAINEERING). It is also known by other names, like the one invented by the American climber Mark Twight, who called it "Death Sport Capital of the World." We could also name it the world capital of ego per square meter, since the city is home—either permanently or for long stretches—to the best specialists of all mountain-related disciplines, from downhill cycling to climbing, not forgetting BASE jumping, parachuting, trail running, ice climbing, extreme skiing, and a long list of etceteras.

Chamonix was the departure point for the first ascent of Mont Blanc in 1786, the feat that gave birth to mountaineering. It was also the town where the mountain guide profession first emerged. With time, Chamonix has adapted to cater to every imaginable mountain activity. Chairlifts, cable cars, and shelters have been built in the city center, so you can plant yourself in just a few minutes on any rock, snow, or ice wall, or in areas where you can fly off in any direction. A system has been created for accessing weather and topographical information on routes that's unique in the world, and the rescue service is flawless.

Evidently, all this has made Chamonix the world university of mountain sports, and the city attracts countless people ready to practice at the highest level possible, twenty-four hours a day, seven days a week. Here, unusual sports are people's daily bread, which results in a mixture of creativity, inflated egos, and cemeteries full of dreamers.

And among these enormous egos was mine, living for years

in a valley where last names like Charlet or Terray were more famous than Kennedy, where social hierarchy was determined by the difficulty of the routes you climbed, and the distinguished elite could be spotted by the silver badge always pinned to their Gore-Tex or the visor of their baseball caps on the hottest days, when it was okay to leave your jacket at home.

In this parallel world of chosen ones, where the valley's real problems, like its enormous pollution, were swept under the carpet of the circus of daily activities and records, I lived and had carved out a space for myself, though I was far from the city's center and social life. In the almost ten years I lived there, I can count the number of friends I made on one hand, and I might only need one more finger to count the days I went into the mountains when I wasn't alone. In any case, in that mountain paradise, I had all the space and desire I needed to progress.

In late June 2013, when the days were long, and the anti-cyclone that had been with us for weeks seemed to be happy where it was and to have no intention of leaving, I was grateful to be spending more time above 4,000 meters than at home. And of course, every day I ran into hundreds of mountaineers, and those ineffable guides who accompany their clients and help them achieve their dream. Since I'd been living there for years, the hostility I'd first encountered as I ran up Mont Blanc or climbed one of the ridges of Bassin du Tour, when they looked me up and down disdainfully and sometimes even insulted me for my way of ascending their mountains, was becoming a thing of the past.

One of the guides I ran into often was Simón Elías Barasoain. He was from La Rioja and had been based in the valley for years, where he alternated the whirlwind of the tourist season with the months when Chamonix became a ghost town, when he fled to remote mountain ranges and tried to open up new climbing routes. For example, the north face of Meru in the Himalayas, or the east face of the Cerro Torre in Patagonia. I'd known him awhile, and not just from what I'd read in magazines about his well-deserved recognition. I met him after running my first Pierra Menta (though I was in the junior category then), when I went to spend four days with other members of the Centro de Tecnificación de Esquí de Montaña, the national youth team, in Chamonix, learning four basic safety concepts, such as what to do if a companion falls into a crevasse or how to rope yourself up to ski on a glacier. We were a dozen excited teenagers, some with our vanity through the roof after stepping down from the podium at Pierra Menta. You know, teenage endorphins . . .

As chance had it, Simón was our guide and coach. On the first day, we took a cable car to Aiguille du Midi, at 3,800 meters. To begin with, it was a mistake not to force us to go on foot, since this would have worn us out a little and given us some lactic acid in our legs, and lowered our endorphin levels. We left the cabin like famished lions who'd just spotted a herd of wounded gazelles. Once we reached the snow, as we put on our skis, Simón tried in his well-intentioned way to explain the key points for skiing a glacier. But we thought we were so smart, and we didn't listen. We just waited impatiently for him to give us a starting signal and competed among ourselves to see who got down first. As soon as Simón gave the order, the stampede began. All of us set out downhill in a straight line, leaning back to keep our balance and feel the snow going by a few centimeters below our asses. And yes, we threw all the safety rules the instructor had explained just a few minutes earlier to the wind. We went down the Vallée Blanche glacier without making a single turn—very good, all parallel—entrusting ourselves to God each time we approached a crevasse, and instead of braking, we tried to pick up more speed to jump over it, watching our companions out of the corners of our eyes and waiting for them to separate, brake, and get left behind. Meanwhile, Simón watched that embarrassing spectacle in terror and astonishment, following us at a distance and begging us loudly to stop acting like idiots.

SIMÓN AND I HADN'T CROSSED PATHS AGAIN UNTIL I MOVED TO Chamonix. Then we met in the mountains often, and though we didn't talk a lot, we wanted to plan some activity that would be a challenge for both of us: for Simón, speed and resistance, and for me, technical difficulty. But the interest we showed on the mountain vanished when we came back down into the valley, where each of us faced the reality of a packed schedule, and as the days went by, we couldn't find a single free one to spend together.

On a Monday in late June, Vivian Bruchez, Sébastien Montaz, and I skied a new route on the east face of Mont Maudit. When we got back to the car around midday, I saw that Simón had sent me a text that said: "Hey, dude, do you feel like doing the Grandes Jorasses on Thursday?" I looked at my schedule. The next day, Tuesday, I had a photo session with a sponsor, on Wednesday I'd arranged to go out with Karl Egloff, and Friday afternoon I was competing in the Chamonix Vertical Kilometer. But on Thursday I was free, so I quickly answered yes. Simón's idea was very simple: climb a mountain like people used to. In other words, run and walk from Chamonix to the foot of a wall neither of us knew, climb a technical route—the Colton-McIntyre—to the summit, and go down the other face to Courmayeur.

Simón and I are polar opposites. He smokes and drinks; I've never smoked in my life, and alcohol doesn't appeal to me at all. He likes the atmosphere of the city, and crowds make me panic. He's crazy about difficult climbs, and I'm crazy about movement. He enjoys taking people up mountains every day, and I'm obsessed with being alone. He thinks sport is a curse, and I can't live without training. Despite our differences in lifestyle, we shared a great passion for the mountains. We had found a small area we agreed on, and we faced it with the excitement of children trying out a new toy.

We'd arranged to meet after dinner on Wednesday in the Montenvers parking lot to choose the equipment we were going to take with us. With our backpacks full, and guided by headlamps, we began our ascent, walking up forest paths where I often ran. When we left the protection of the trees, a magnificent spectacle unfurled before us: on that pale night, the starlight shone and lit up the faces of the peaks around us. The Grandes Jorasses awaited us, covered in a film of intense and dazzling whiteness. Was this a sign that the snow was hard and we could climb up quickly and safely, or was it a fresh, inconsistent, powdery snow that scarcely covered the rocks? With this doubt internalized, we went on across the Mer de Glace, an ice field that was once kilometers long but has gradually lost hundreds of cubic meters each year and now wears an oversized name, since it would be more fitting to call it a tongue or a pool of ice instead of a sea. In one of the streams that cross the ice field, we stocked up on water—a liter for Simón and half a liter for me. That was likely enough to get us to the other side of the mountain.

When we reached the foot of the wall, the shadow of 1,200 meters of rock enveloped us in thick darkness. In the middle of the night, in a place like this, our feeling of smallness and insignificance became even more intense. We lost a few hours going up and down the base of the wall, dotted with spurs and channels, looking for the route we wanted to use to go up, the Colton-McIntyre route. In the end, just as it began to get light, we found the blue ice slopes that allowed us to start the ascent at a good pace up the first third of the wall. When day had set in, a cold air peeled the sleep from our eyes, suddenly reminding us that we were right in the middle of the north face. When the difficult part began, the climb was much more static, since we were starting to belay each other, and a bitter cold seeped into our bones. Meanwhile, we imagined the runners in tank tops at the bottom of the valley and the climbers suffocating from heat on the sunny walls.

"Damn it, Simón, yesterday was so great . . . with the warmth of the sun, over 4,000 meters, climbing all day in our T-shirts, and with those amazing views . . . Why the fuck do we always have to go somewhere cold?" I grumbled sarcastically.

"Yeah, we could have been getting tanned and handsome down south, and here we are, quaking with cold and fear. But if you look at in another way, if this weather refreshes our bodies, imagine how it'll refresh our souls!"

Simón has the gift of words, of succinct and spot-on answers— a gift that, if you have it, makes you the king of dinner parties.

Not long ago I had read his book *Alpinismo Bisexual y Otros Escritos de Altura* (*Bisexual Mountain Climbing and Other Writings of Height*), a sharp and entertaining collection, though I can tell you completely sincerely that what grabbed my attention in the bookstore was its cover. It's an amateur photo of the author himself, skinny, with hairy legs and a beard, stark naked except for a thong and some climbing boots, plus a headband and some sunglasses, striking a pose like an eighties porn actor. And all this, for the love of God, in the middle of a Patagonian glacier, with all his climbing equipment and food in what looks like a bivouac scattered around him. Pure dynamite.

He contemplates everything he does through a satirical lens, and says that his work as a mountain guide is unique since it consists of putting people in danger in order to save them. As I spend time with him, I understand his passion for what he does and the way he manages to convey his feelings at each moment as he climbs, with barely any need for explanations. And how he preserves his authentic mountaineer spirit, explaining to his clients that what matters isn't reaching the summit but what you experience along the way, whether or not you achieve your goal.

Simón tells me that his book is an "ode to failure," since "in mountain climbing there are so many heroic tales about epic ascents and life-or-death challenges to reach a summit, but we all know that ninety-nine percent of the time you don't actually reach the summit. There's no heroism, because that's not what mountain climbing is about. It's bisexual, it's about optimizing all the resources available, and usually ending up not setting foot on the summit, but that doesn't mean you've failed. Quite the opposite."

We continued our climb, and the words we exchanged were brief. If one of us belayed the other, we exchanged the occasional comment about the beauty of our surroundings or the difficulty of the stretch we'd just climbed, and with no further ado, we passed each other the equipment and separated again. When we climbed with a tense rope, advancing at the same time, with 60 meters of rope between us, we communicated via the cord that connected us. If the rope stopped, that meant it was a difficult stretch; if it went backward, it meant we were going the wrong way; if it advanced slowly, we were tired; if it was getting tugged, either we'd arrived somewhere or we needed to move more slowly.

Climbing with Simón, I felt at ease. Although we wanted to move steadily and not waste any time, he didn't hesitate to look for the best placement for each anchor, and when I heard him huff and puff because he couldn't find the route, he soon discovered a way to move forward, calmly and with a smile on his face.

Ten hours after we began the climb, the sun skimmed our faces as we reached the summit, and we had to strip down quickly due to the heat coming up from the south. We could have done with a little of this to melt the thin layer of snow that had hid the path and made the climb so difficult all morning!

Suddenly, our bodies relaxed in the heat, knowing that the most difficult part was over. The first thing to loosen up was our stomachs. "Ouch, what a bellyache!" We looked at each other, and sure that there was no one for miles around, we took down our pants and emptied out all of what had been with us through the night and into the morning.

"Have you ever taken a shit with a better view?"

And we both burst out laughing as we gazed at the Alps from on high.

AS USUAL, AFTER THE TWENTY-THREE HOURS OUR SHARED EXPEDI-
tion lasted, each of us went back to our schedules, and summer ran its course, erasing events as we achieved them. And we couldn't find a single page with a gap for any of the expeditions we'd planned as we descended to Courmayeur, on the trail following the scent of the pizzas awaiting us.

Simón put his mountain guide uniform back on and, with the same calm and patience as ever, kept teaching lessons of love for the mountains to hundreds of clients wanting to climb peaks like Mont Blanc. All of them learned so much that in the end they knew the summit they'd been chasing wasn't what mattered most. Maybe guides like Simón do have godlike qualities since they can light the way for others through their love of the mountains, and they initiate new climbers on a path of sacrifice and fulfillment.

For my part, the day after sharing that truly amazing experience with Simón, I put a number on my back and went on with my usual procession of summer events.

Ueli

I was lost in the narrow streets of Ringgenberg, a tiny town near Interlaken, Switzerland, still full of rural charm and the smell of nature. Unlike the neighboring villages and stations in France, it hasn't become overcrowded, and its inhabitants haven't massacred the architecture. The streets are all paved with cobblestones, and the houses are built from polished, round logs, with a maximum of two stories, all the windows and balconies bursting with flowers of many colors, not a single wilted petal to spoil the effect. Water flows abundantly from the fountain in the central plaza, and old men spend the afternoons sitting on benches and chatting.

I'd been past the fountain twice and hadn't found the house I was looking for. In the end, I stopped the car and rolled down the window to ask an old man, "Excuse me, do you know where Ueli Steck lives?" I couldn't quite understand the answer he gave in Swiss German, but I could decipher his gestures well enough to be satisfied.

I reached the door to Ueli's house, called him, and he came out to tell me where to park. We then jumped into gear, and ten minutes was enough to get all the equipment we needed ready to climb the north face of the Eiger the following morning. When we were finished, we had a dish of pasta with parmesan for dinner.

The first time I heard any mention of Ueli Steck was around 2007, when I read in a magazine that in less than four hours he'd done the climb we were about to repeat. The next year, he destroyed his own record by climbing it in less than three. Compared with that, what we were getting ready to do was just some simple training for him. I, on the other hand, was overwhelmed by a mixture of excitement and respect. I was also afraid of looking ridiculous next to a man who'd scaled the wall we were about to climb thirty-nine times.

A few weeks earlier, we had met in the Himalayas. I'd had twelve days of vacation between the end of the trail-running season and a trip to present products for a sponsor in Southeast Asia, and I took the chance for a recreational trip to Khumbu, the Nepalese region home to emblematic mountains like Everest, Lhotse, and Ama Dablam. I stopped in Kathmandu for a few hours to secure my trekking permits, took a flight straight to Lukla, and, as soon as I arrived, set off running with my small backpack, which had everything I needed for a long week in the mountains. After a few days in the valleys of Gokyo and on the summit of Lobuche, I reached Chukhung, the last village in the valley that leads to the south faces of Lhotse and Nuptse, at an altitude of almost 5,000 meters. I went straight to the Pemba lodge, which I knew from my other trips, and when I walked into the dining room, I saw Ueli Steck and Hélias Mille-rioux. They told me they'd already been there awhile, acclimating and waiting for the right conditions to try to climb the south face of Nuptse Alpine style—which means without using any fixed ropes, altitude camps, assistance, or porters, carrying all of what is needed for the climb on your shoulders. Meanwhile, they were taking advantage of the opportunity to run and climb in the surrounding area.

I like Khumbu for the training opportunities it has to offer. You can do 6,000- and 7,000-meter mountains, like in the Alps, climbing 3,000 or 4,000. The villages are 5,000 meters up and have everything you need to live and to train: beds with blankets, rooms with fireplaces to shelter from the cold nights, plenty of food, and even, if you're in Dingboche, delicious chocolate croissants straight out of a wood-fired oven.

One day I went out with Hélias and Ueli, and we traveled in sneakers to the foot of one of the unnamed 6,000-meter peaks nearby. When we reached the snow, we put on our crampons and started to climb a sharp, rocky ridge with incredible views of the immense wall of rock that forms the south face of Lhotse and Nuptse. Makalu was right beside us, and we were surrounded by hundreds of slender pyramids of snow. We reached the highest point and, after a brief pause, began to descend the shaded side. Since we hadn't brought any rope, we kept a good distance between us as we descended, to avoid throwing snow on top of each other. I followed in Ueli's footprints, amazed at how he could manage with just one ice axe. I took my second ice axe out of my backpack and climbed down to the glacier. I caught up with him, and while we waited for Hélias, he asked me if I'd ever been to Grindelwald, Switzerland. I told him I hadn't. He wanted to know if I'd ever climbed the Eiger. I told him no. He suggested that we do it one day. I said yes.

The next day, I had to leave in a rush to catch the plane that would take me to Kuala Lumpur. After a few days of roaming around enormous Asian cities, I returned to a regular autumn in the French station of Tignes, where I made the most of the snow and altitude by starting to ski and getting in as much training as I could before the snow arrived near home. We call this "doing the hamster" on the ski slopes—up and down, up and down, without getting off the wheel, tediously counting the hours and the meters.

One of those days, on my way back from training, after I'd completely forgotten about Ueli, I received a message from him. "Hi. Conditions look great on Eiger. I'm free tomorrow." *Wow!* I glanced up from my phone and quickly assessed what was scattered around in my car: some crampons, an ice axe, and a light harness. *This won't be enough.* Luckily Chamonix was nearby and I was able to stock up on everything else I needed.

WHILE MOST PEOPLE I'VE GONE INTO THE MOUNTAINS WITH HAVE HAD a hard time taking unnecessary items out of their backpack to lighten their load, with Ueli, it was the opposite. After packing up a 30-meter rope with some quickdraws, a couple of ice screws, and half a liter of water, our twenty-liter backpacks were half empty and we wondered what we were forgetting. What took the longest was deciding which boots and crampons to take. When I went to the Grandes Jorasses with Simón, I wore some waterproof sneakers whose flexibility made the approach more pleasant, and when I added rigid crampons, they stayed relatively firm for climbing on ice. This saved me from having to lug heavy climbing boots around in my backpack. Though the invention worked and gave me ideas for designing some new footwear prototypes, I did suffer on the steepest ice slopes from a lack of stability. Ueli wanted to see how that invention would work on the Eiger, but in the end, we decided it would be better to take both light sneakers and climbing boots. The crampon-sneaker concept would have to wait until some other time.

The next day we left early. We set out running across the fields, and the cows held it against us, since they'd been sleeping in peace before we'd arrived. Though Ueli knew these trails as if he'd grown up running along them, he'd never set out running from Grindelwald to climb the Eiger, since there's a cog railway than can take you to the foot of the wall. His passion came from when he used to do technical climbing, attempting increasingly difficult walls and opening up new routes. When he looked at a mountain, what he really saw was the wall, the straightest part; the rest of the mountain held no special interest. Despite his preferences, when I had suggested we set out running from town, he was excited.

We ran up at a good pace, and as we adjusted to the day's rhythm, we continued our conversation from the night before.

When Ueli asked me about training and nutrition for long-distance races, I took refuge in the certainty of my answers to get the uncertainty of what would happen later off my mind, when we would trade the comfort of a sixty-degree slope for the challenges of a vertical climb. Ueli wanted to know if our pace was good, and I told him not to worry, that he was a great runner, that many professional runners would love to have his twenty-second place in the OCC (Orsières-Champex-Chamonix), the UTMB's 56-kilometer sister race.

"Don't you believe it," he answered. "I got there an hour after Marc Pinsach, the guy who came in first, at eighteen percent of his time. I'm not a runner, but I want to train to get faster, and I also want to run hundred-kilometer races."

I could tell by the look in his eyes that he was imagining what that could bring to his future mountain projects, and I encouraged him, saying that judging by how he was running on this trail, it wouldn't be hard for him to do long distance if he applied himself and trained well.

"You know what?" he continued. "I don't buy it, that idea that you can improve just by climbing and doing mountains. A lot of mountain climbers just climb and don't train. If they have some free time, to give you an example, they use it to do an interesting climb, but it doesn't even occur to them to go running or go to the gym, and they don't do any anaerobic exercise. I know if I want to achieve all the projects I have in mind, I need to train really hard in all those activities so I can be successful at the riskiest, most difficult climbs."

It's not easy to find someone like Ueli, not just among mountain climbers but among athletes in general, who took disciplined training so seriously. Every day of the year, he followed the guide-lines of an Olympic trainer, and it was interesting to observe the similarities and differences between his activity and my own.

"What I do is divide the season into stages," I told him, "but since every year my goals are scheduled around the same time—skiing from January to April, running from May to September—it's easy to set up a routine. That way I know in advance that fall is when I need to focus on volume, and the beginning of winter I need to work on intensity, and I keep going like that, following the blocks I've set up."

"I train in blocks, too," he explained, "but they're not fixed by the time of year. Instead, I set them depending on what I'm working toward at the time. For example, if my goal is to go to California and free-climb El Capitán, I do a few specific months of strength training and sport climbing beforehand, with a week of distance training in between, so I don't lose any muscle mass. If the goal is a huge wall in the Himalayas, I spend a block focusing on resistance training, with a lot of slopes with easy terrain, and a few weeks of technical training mixed in."

In any case, Ueli was a guy who trained for twelve hundred hours a year, a figure like those of cross-country skiing or cycling world champions. Just like my terrain for doing the hamster in autumn is the ski slopes of Tignes, Ueli paid homage to that cute little metaphorical animal on the north face of the Eiger.

We were talking so much that we almost didn't notice we'd arrived at the foot of the wall. It had taken us just over two hours to get there. I looked up for the first time since we'd left and allowed myself to be intimidated by the 800 meters of black rock. Despite being the smaller of the three mountains in the massif, the Eiger is the most feared. It stands beside two other peaks, the Jungfrau (virgin) and the Mönch (monk), each of which inspires respect. The name of the mountain in front of me doesn't lie: the Eiger, the ogre.

We took off our sneakers and put on our boots and crampons. Without wasting any more time at the foot of the wall, we began to climb up some relatively easy sheets of rock, and after passing some steep patches of snow, we reached the halfway point. This was where the real difficulties would begin. With a little imagination, if we wanted to go down now, we could ski. With a little imagination, I repeat. But on our way up, everything would be vertical.

We roped ourselves a few meters apart and kept climbing together, placing the occasional anchor when the terrain was more vertical. Meter by meter, the anxiety of not being able to climb with skill started to disappear, and I got caught up in enjoying myself and feeling playful. Our path was very long, almost 3 kilometers, and we traversed the wall from right to left for numerous stretches, on terrain where the difficulties never lasted long. Small cliffs of 20 or 30 vertical meters of ice or rock gave way to simpler snowy slopes, which, hanging over the void, imparted an intimidating sense of exposure.

The two of us were alone on the wall, and though we had to start opening a trail, Ueli knew it so well that he didn't hesitate for a moment when determining which way to go, and as we pressed forward, he showed me the routes he'd already climbed.

"Here's Jeff Lowe's Metanoia route. I tried it a few years ago. And there are Patience and the Young Spider, which I established myself years ago."

"Ueli, is there anything you haven't done on this wall?"

"Oof, a whole lot of things . . . Even if I did a wall a day, I'm in my forties now and I'm getting old, so I see them all with different eyes. Look, even today, I'd never set out running from Grindelwald to climb up here."

"Maybe one day you should try skiing down from here," I said to rib him, knowing he wasn't a fan of skiing.

"Well, I've never done it with skis, but I did a couple of descents to train for Annapurna."

"What . . . ?" I let slip in amazement. "But . . . but . . . that wall is already pretty hard to climb up, and getting down is even more complicated on technical terrain!"

"Well, I wanted to make sure I could climb back down a technical stretch and on a large wall, so I'd have the resources and confidence when I went to the Himalayas. That's why I thought a good way to train would be to go up the west face, the easiest one, and climb down the north face, which I know from memory and can do with my eyes closed."

I was so amazed to hear him talk such nonsense that I couldn't even think of an answer. He kept talking about this and that, saying that actually the south face of Annapurna wasn't any more difficult than this wall, and was therefore easy to climb down. Incredible. I tried to absorb what he'd just told me as we kept climbing.

In fact, a couple of years earlier, when Ueli completed a solitary climb that included 2,000 meters of wall on the south face of Annapurna, ending at 8,901 meters, the whole world was stunned. That wall presents enormous difficulties, and the altitude imposes additional obstacles. He had climbed it alone and in a single twenty-eight-hour burst. A few weeks later, the French mountain climbers Stéphane Benoist and Yannick Graziani did the same route. It took them ten days from start to finish, and there were many complications due to the altitude and cold, which eventually led to the amputation of four fingers.

Ueli's account of his climb was jaw-dropping.

"While I climbed, I was completely detached from the world. Nothing existed except the climb. The idea of past or future had disappeared, and I was just in the here and now. A stab with the ice axe, then another, one step, then another. All I could see was the ice axes penetrating the snow and ice. My vision narrowed. There I was, in the middle of a gigantic wall, with very little equipment. I felt light but very exposed. I knew if I made a mistake, no matter how small, I'd be dead. And despite all that, I wasn't afraid I would make a mistake. I gave myself orders. I was in control of the person climbing the south face of Annapurna. I didn't feel myself. If that person fell, it wouldn't bother me. Because the future didn't exist."

He had practically experienced the beyond. Before setting out, he'd accepted that his path went in only one direction. He'd accepted that he might end up dead. Once he made it down alive and kicking, a void took hold of his spirit, the kind of void that fills everything when you're convinced you've reached a limit you'll never be able to surpass. When you've experienced that limit.

Ueli had to deal with criticism from people who cast doubt on his feat since he couldn't document it with photos. "Oh, I'm sorry, all-night climbing, dodging the wind and the rockfalls without my camera because I lost it in a little avalanche on the wall." Within the professional community, no one had any doubt about his climb, and he was awarded the Piolet d'Or (Golden Ice Axe), the prize for the best mountain-climbing activity of the year. Even so, for a while he was bothered by the criticism and lack of understanding.

"But what does anyone know about what it means to solo climb a wall like that?" he said. "How can they imagine the decisions I made if they've never climbed in such an exposed situation?"

Every once in a while this happens: when someone imagines and goes through with something the whole world believes impossible, rather than feeling inspired, many people shut off in denial. It's easier to say no than to recognize your own limits.

But all wounds heal with time. At least, that's what they say. Ueli had gotten his motivation back by doing all the peaks over 4,000 meters in the Alps in a row, climbing in the Himalayas again, and training to improve in other areas. No matter how many times he told me, I couldn't believe what he promised his wife: that he would never solo climb an extremely difficult route again.

"Even though I told Nicole I wouldn't," he said, "I can climb the Eiger fast and without any risk."

THAT DAY, THE WEATHER WAS FANTASTIC. THERE WAS NO WIND, AND it was warm—bearing in mind that we were on a north face and almost 4,000 meters up. This meant we could climb in a jacket and gloves, and fully enjoy the ascent. As we climbed, he constantly observed the wall's conditions and talked enthusiastically about different strategies, telling me his ideas for lighter materials, or for getting food and drink more efficiently in order to pick up the pace. It was priceless to watch Ueli move around this terrain. He looked like he was ascending along a flat path. I watched him assess the ice quality, noticing how easily he carried out all the movements. I tried to absorb everything I saw and everything he explained. This is my favorite kind of mountain, because the difficulties demand concentration and present a certain amount of risk, but they aren't so huge that you have to stop and climb one at a time so as not to slip up at any step. In a couple of more complicated stretches, Ueli belayed me by running the rope around my back, and we kept climbing at a good pace until we reached the final crevices, where he practically broke into a run, even though the terrain was still tricky. I followed him as best I could, a few meters behind, with the rope nice and taut. I copied his movements but had no time to see where to put my hands and feet. Ice axe on ice, crampon on rock, ice axe on rock, crampon on ice. After a while, we found ourselves on the highest ridge.

In the green fields 2,000 meters below, the cows we had annoyed that morning were grazing peacefully. It was midday, just seven hours after we had left Grindelwald, when we started heading down the other side of the mountain. For me, today's climb had been a first-class experience, but for Ueli it was just part of his regular training. I was grateful to him for this master class in mountain climbing. It took us less than two hours to get down the east face, and we passed in front of the cable car. We put our sneakers back on and took off running toward the car. It had been ten hours since we left it. I bought a couple of drinks and some cookies. We scarfed them down and exchanged some equipment. He put on some shorts and headed off to a rock wall in the Interlaken area to do some sport climbing. I was going to Tignes. I would have time for another ascent in the afternoon.

Four days went by, packed with intense training, before I got another text message from Ueli: "Today it was great conditions. 2 hours 22 minutes ;)."

Solo

I go up and down glaciers and count the days in thousands of meters.

After I came back from the Eiger, an idea lodged in my head and kept growing as I racked up training hours, almost of its own accord. The weather had been good for a week, and cold, which meant the mountain conditions were probably still good for climbing. After everything I had learned from Simón in June and from Ueli a few days ago, I wanted to complete my personal trilogy by putting it into practice for myself. For me, solo climbing is the most direct and authentic. It's just you, with your doubts and fears. You write your destiny with your decisions alone.

I went back to my apartment with tired legs after spending the morning training. I glanced at the weather forecast. I saw on Google Maps that it was a five-hour drive to Zermatt, at the foot of Matterhorn. That sounded about right. I let the friends I train with know that they shouldn't wait for me the next day. I loaded up the truck with everything I needed. Then I made a little pasta with olive oil and went straight to sleep.

DAWN CAME, AND I DROVE TO ZERMATT, WHERE I SAW A FEW TOUR-ists looking like zombies, wandering around on the verge of a drunken coma, trying to find the hotel where they'd booked a thousand-euro room for the night. I drove through the streets and stopped at the exit to the Patrouille des Glaciers. This time there weren't two thousand runners behind me and I didn't feel the excitement of having to compete, but I breathed in the same energy, now that I was leaving the town to head toward the valleys.

At midmorning, I reached the Hörnli refuge, where I drank some water and ate the four cookies I'd brought. As I changed from sneakers to boots, I noticed that no one had stayed in the free refuge overnight. This meant there wouldn't be any rope teams up where I was headed. Without wasting any time, I set out to look for the foot of the wall. The temperature was good. Not so cold that I'd have a rough time, and not so warm that detached rocks or ice would give me any trouble.

I headed up the sixty-degree slope of snow and ice. I was doing well and moving quickly, almost running along this terrain, and I felt comfortable. When I got to the foot of the ramp, a kind of rock and ice gully, I was surprised to see that it was completely dry, and I had some doubts. It was going to be tougher than I thought. *But that's what I came for, right? So I'd have to make decisions like this one* . . . I decided to keep going. I was carrying a thin 30-meter rope and some equipment that I could leave behind, or that would be helpful if I had to rappel down or belay myself in case I decided to keep going. I started climbing up the ramp, placing the ice axes and crampons delicately in the cracks in the black schist. After about 100 relatively easy meters, I came upon a more vertical chimney formation. I climbed a couple of meters more, but I couldn't see how to position myself to keep going safely, and when I looked down, I realized the fall would be . . . No, falling wasn't an option. I climbed down a few meters until I found a well-placed piton. I reinforced it by hammering it farther in with an ice axe, and when it seemed firm, I took the rope from my backpack and tied one of the ends to my harness, threaded the rope through the hole in the piton, and tied the rope back on to the harness with a slipknot. I gave myself more rope as I climbed, and hoped the piton would be able to resist the jolt if I fell. If not, I figured the 20- or 30-meter drop wouldn't do me too much harm and I could either climb back up or back down. So, I measured my pace as if I weren't in a harness. Little by little, the stress diminished. I picked the rope back up and kept climbing the ramp, which at this point had ice beneath a layer of powdery snow. At least now I could drive my crampons and ice axes into something that made me feel safe.

Three hours later, I emerged on the ridge near the summit. It had been an intense climb and had taken maximum concentration, and when I left the wall I felt a rush of adrenaline as the energy left my body.

With the days shorter in fall, it was midafternoon by the time I reached the metal cross that someone had planted at the summit of Matterhorn. I looked down and saw the peak's shadow beginning to lengthen over the valleys. I wished it were summer so I could see the clean ridges without snow. A couple of years before, it had taken me only fifty-six minutes to get down to the town of Cervinia from this spot. This time it looked like it would be much longer and trickier, since it was covered in ice and snow and there were no markers indicating which path to take for a quick descent.

I climbed down cautiously as the shadow of Matterhorn

continued to lengthen toward the east, casting an immense arrow that showed me which way to go. I was trapped by the night. I turned on my headlamp and looked for a better path. The terrain on the ridge isn't complicated, but it is exposed, and in these conditions I couldn't go jumping from rock to rock, even though I felt safe and I was going at a good pace.

Suddenly, I felt my right crampon catch on something on my left leg. My body slowly lurched forward. I tried to free my foot to step ahead, but it was caught on my pants. There was nothing I could do. My body plunged into the void and I turned upside down. I felt the first impact when I landed on my shoulders, then tumbled down even farther into the darkness. I couldn't see myself. The second blow hit me on the back.

I've been convinced I was living the last seconds of my life on two occasions. This was the first. I thought everything was ending right there. As I fell, all I could do was murmur "Shit" in a low voice, as if not wanting to disturb anyone, but I was angry at myself. I thought of nothing except resisting the impact however I could, and then tried stretching my arms out to grab on to anything to avoid what seemed inevitable.

With one of those movements, my arm got trapped between some rocks and I managed to break my fall. I got up as best I could. My whole body was shaking, and I was breathing heavily from adrenaline. I couldn't decide whether to scream at the top of my lungs or to merge with my surroundings and completely disappear. After taking a minute to recover from the fright, I did a quick check of my injuries. My elbow had suffered the first blow and was semi-dislocated, but since that was nothing new for me, I quickly clicked it back into place. My legs had been hit a number of times, and I had a small wound right where the crampon had gotten caught on my pant leg. None of this seemed too serious, so I could keep going down. With the first few steps, I noticed my legs were shaking, and so I dropped my butt to the ground to scoot forward. Gradually, I returned to a normal pace.

Ten and a half hours after setting out, I was back in Zermatt. I bought a slice of pizza in a supermarket to eat on my way back to Tignes.

Stéphane

But good luck isn't always on your side.

In the year 2000, when I was twelve years old, I was at the Malniu refuge in La Cerdanya, just like every summer. I spent half my school vacations there, helping my father. I made sandwiches and eggs and beans, brewed coffee, folded blankets, swept the rooms or set the dinner table for the mountaineers who were doing the GR 11 or going to see the lakes. Working in a refuge means getting up early and going to bed late, because breakfast is served at dawn and you have to leave everything tidy at night, but between the first meal of the day and the time people start arriving at midday, there's a decent stretch. My sister and I made use of it to race in the area around the refuge, not running but climbing up the walls, grabbing on to the handholds between the stone blocks. In the afternoons, while we waited to serve dinner, if it was cold we lit the woodstove and flipped through the many magazines lying around in the dining room. When I saw the cover of an issue of *Desnivel* with a photo of a skier on a steep slope, all bundled up, but with his legs bare, my jaw dropped. The headline read, "Davo Karničar Skis Everest."

"Whoa, check this out!" I yelled to my sister, thrusting the magazine in her face. "Do you really think you can ski down Everest?"

We started looking through the pages, where the article explained in more detail how Davo had managed it, and I was astonished by the Slovenian skier's tenacity and technique. I had not yet done a steep descent myself, but for some reason I was convinced I would die skiing down the K2 at the age of twenty-one.

At the end of that same summer, I began to compete in alpine skiing (it was still called this, before the name changed to ski mountaineering), and for years I forgot about Davo and impossible descents. My school folder was decorated with two photos, one of Kenenisa Bekele, who was winning all the races between 5,000 and 10,000 meters, and one of Stéphane Brosse in an alpine ski competition, about to take a new step, mid-ascent, eyes fixed on the peaks, perhaps anticipating the movements that would win him another race—the European Cup in Morgins, Switzerland, where I would eventually make my international debut.

In 2007, Stéphane was retiring from international competitions, and I was just beginning to compete with adults. The French skier became a high-end spectator who came to cheer us on for the four days we fought to win the Pierra Menta. A year later, I decided to leave the Pyrenees and live in the Alps, and two friends—Mireia Miró and Laëtitia Roux—and I found a small wood chalet at the end of a road in the Aravis, from which we could walk out the door with our skis and climb the steep foothills of mountains like Étale and Charvin. Stéphane lived in a neighboring town, and this was also his natural terrain. I used to see him on the mountains, swift and precise, just as I remembered him from his glory days in the competitions.

In 2012, I began the Summits of My Life project, and I wanted to talk to Stéphane right away since we shared a vision of going into the mountains quickly and always in motion. My first challenge consisted of crossing the Mont Blanc massif, skiing from east to west and summiting the main peaks; to do so I would have to tackle some difficult descents. He was a brilliant downhill skier. When he competed, you could see the difference in his descents, which he approached with sublime technique, and he knew how to read the terrain like nobody else. After putting his numbers away in a drawer, he carried out some of the most dizzying descents ever seen. Along with Pierre Tardivel, he successfully broke the record of the descent from Nant Blanc to Aiguille Verte without rappelling. Stéphane was the first to use very light competition equipment that allowed him to do rapid ascents on that terrain, opening the door to a succession of previously unimagined ascent techniques. For me, the project of crossing Mont Blanc was in embryonic form, but when I mentioned it to Stéphane, he told me it had been on his mind for some time. He unfolded some maps of the area on the floor and told me with total precision where we'd be able to cross.

WE WENT OUT TOGETHER A NUMBER OF TIMES IN PREPARATION, AND he introduced me to the world of *esquí de pendiente*, or "incline skiing." First, we went to the north face of the Courtes, the Barbey de l'Aiguille d'Argentière, the north face of the Dômes de Miage, and the Droites. Hardly saying a word, he gradually taught me to tackle those downhill slopes. I can't say for sure that Stéphane was the world's most sensible mentor. He always had some problem with the equipment, but his angelic technique allowed him to go down with only one ski or a broken boot, without anyone being able to tell the difference from when he was fully equipped. And in those circumstances, I had my hands full just keeping up with him.

When the conditions looked good, we attempted the crossing. A few weeks earlier, we'd done a similar one in the Aravis, and we were feeling strong. We spent that week skiing in the area to finish assessing the conditions we'd find on the mountain. Our crossing ended in the worst way we could have imagined. After over twenty hours of happiness, as we looked for an entry point for the final descent, a ledge on the summit of the Aiguille d'Argentière collapsed, taking Stéphane with it.

Vivian

In the months after Stéphane's death, I dealt with the guilt by bingeing on alcohol and taking insane risks in the mountains. Luckily, a few friends helped me to redirect those dangerous urges toward a more constructive kind of calm. These friends were Séb Montaz and Vivian Bruchez, who'd been recording us in the Aravis and on the Mont Blanc crossing, and also Jordi Tosas.

Vivian and I had met only a few times before. Though we'd crossed paths when he was recording, we'd never climbed or skied together, and that was why I was surprised to get a call from him at the end of October in 2012.

"How's it going, Kilian? I saw you went to Chardonnet today. How's the snow looking?"

"Good. I went up the usual way. There's quite a lot, but it's pretty stable. I'd say the conditions are good." I was trying not to make a mistake talking to someone who knew those mountains a thousand times better than I did.

"And did you see the north face? Was it white or did it look icy?"

"Mmm . . . well, I think it was pretty white. I'm not a hundred percent sure, but that's how it seemed." I tried to remember how it looked. I'd gone over it, but I hadn't paid much attention.

"Okay, thanks," he said, and we said goodbye.

After a while, I got a message. "Want to come and ski the Migot Spur tomorrow?" I replied yes without thinking twice, and we agreed to meet the next morning at the foot of the mountain. Then I realized I didn't have any skis that were wider than competition skis, with the bindings mounted, and none of the ones I had were in very good shape. I looked for some boards and bindings I had lying around at home and went straight to the store to get them mounted.

For me, Chardonnet is a special mountain. It isn't as well known as the other peaks around Chamonix, but the fact that you can't get to it by cable car, that it's a totem rising up in the first row from the valley, and that there's no particularly easy route to climb it make it an especially appealing challenge. Stéphane had climbed practically all of the possible routes and had told me it was his favorite mountain in the whole range. On the different faces of that mountain, after Stéphane, Vivian opened up a new world of possibilities for me, offering me a perspective that would change the way I saw mountains forever.

Vivian wasn't much older than me, but he had much more experience with *esquí de pendiente*, and with that kind of terrain. But he always considered me an equal when it came to making decisions, and he trained me just like my mother did when she made us find our way home. When I'm by his side, I always have a sense of safety and control bordering on serenity, since he distances the activity from extreme feelings, eliminating words like *risk* and *fear* from his vocabulary and replacing them with *pleasure* and *happiness.*

After that descent of the Migot, there were others, and also repetitions, from the Mont Blanc range to Alaska and the Himalayas, but Vivian and I occasionally went back to Chardonnet. For a few years he'd been visualizing a line on the mountain's west face, a face covered in spurs of red granite that offered excellent rock for climbing in summer. And letting his imagination play, he found it was possible to link some small snow corridors with strips of rock that ran from the summit all the way to the foot of the wall, almost completely continuously.

At the end of December 2015, we made our first attempt. We made it onto the wall too late, and due to its multiple exposures, the snow changed consistency at different speeds, increasing the difficulty. The second time we went was Christmas. The mountain gave us the gift of a perfect day with blue sky and no wind. We were also alone in the valley, which is normally crowded. It must have been because it was December 25. While most people were at home carving a chicken or a turkey and simmering the gravy, we were out looking for answers on the east wall of Chardonnet, at almost 4,000 meters' altitude. We climbed to the summit and made the descent on that face of the mountain in an interesting combination of snow skiing and dry skiing, a term Vivian came up with to describe climbing downhill with skis on your feet. When we reached a spot where the snow ended or dwindled so much that, according to logic, we should set up a rappel, we kept going down with our skis on, supporting them against the rock, and as if they were crampons or climbing shoes, we climbed down with the help of our hands or ice axes until we reached the next snowy stretch.

While at first this technique helped us avoid taking out the rope and leaving things on the mountain, there came a point when dry skiing demanded so much concentration and imagination that the time we spent looking for and executing the movements was twice what we would have needed to set up a good rappel. It was probably a completely absurd exercise, since with difficulties like that, it's faster and safer to put on a harness and abseil down, or sling the skis onto your back and climb down with crampons on your feet. In any case, it was our absurdity. In the end, isn't it just as absurd to take a complicated route up a mountain when you could also climb an easier and safer way? And by the same token, isn't it pointless to climb mountains in the first place?

The path we'd opened up wasn't the one Vivian had imagined, the one that had captivated him for a long time. We had to wait until the next spring for the conditions to be right to try again. Right after the last stage of the Pierra Menta, which Mathéo Jacquemoud and I won, I got another message. "Cheers, you're an artist! Congrats! Do you feel like trying Chardonnet on Tuesday?"

The next Sunday was the last event in the Skyrunning World Cup. I came in first. With time, however, I've learned that you have to leave rest until later, especially if you have a chance to spend a good day in the mountains. And the descent Vivian was proposing would be worth it.

When we climbed the route we'd imagined we would come down by, we realized how beautiful the line was. It wasn't an *esquí de pendiente* descent to be valued for how steep it was. Or for its length. Or for the trickiness of the dry-ski approach. Or for the climb. It was a journey on skis across an enormous mountain wall. The words *ski* and *mountaineering* carry all the meaning. It was a five-hour celebration of sensations that culminated in a sunset just as we reached the glacier again. We were slaves to movement who had achieved the fluidity to swerve down a half-moon-shaped stretch of snow in the middle of the red granite wall of a mountain.

EVEREST IN
WINTER

When you think of Nepal, what comes to mind are majestic mountains, tropical forests, and rustic villages scattered across silent valleys. But my first steps there were permeated with insufferable heat, dusty air, the stench of pollution, and the racket of thousands of cars horns honking all at once. I was in the midst of all this, bewildered by the chaos, when Jordi Tosas and Jordi Corominas, who'd been waiting for me at the airport, grabbed me by the hand to rescue me and took me off to discover the enormous mountains. It was February 2012.

We went alone to a valley on the border of Nepal and Tibet, and for four weeks we became part of the landscape of mountains that touch the sky, higher than the so-called death zone. We skied slopes covered in powder, climbed massive walls of ice, and walked across endless moraines to reach the highest points. We didn't reach any summits, but on our journeys up the mountains and their walls, with every attempt and at every step, I learned more than ever before. I learned that simplicity is the hardest thing to learn in this world of inhuman dimensions, since it's the purest form of commitment and discomfort.

The expedition can be summarized quickly: three guys, three backpacks, three pairs of skis, a small tent, a spoon for sharing food, and one freeze-dried meal a day for the three of us. All this to spend a month in the mountains, where they taught me what the Himalayas were really like—solitary, distant, and deserted—where our presence left no trace but some footprints in the snow, which disappeared after a few hours, melted by the sun or buried under a fresh dusting of powder. They taught me that if you want to climb as simply as possible, the way the Jordis recommended, all you really need—to climb any mountain in the world—fits into a forty-liter backpack. I ended up filling that backpack to the brim with other treasures: the silences between the few words they spoke—you could fill an encyclopedia with them—and the idea that less is more, and doing something means nothing, but how you do it means everything.

SOME MOUNTAINEERS ARE DETERMINED NOT TO LET THE SPORT evolve. They're like a kind of mountain Amish who reject the technology offered by technical progress and the new equipment that lets us climb mountains more easily. These traditionalists won't take cable cars to the summit or grab on to fixed ropes in the mountains to avoid plunging to their deaths. They refuse to rely on bottled oxygen, which would allow them to climb better, and choose to stay in a cramped tent eating freeze-dried food when they could be in a camp equipped with comforts like internet and delicious food. And all this just because they don't want to be packed into a helicopter to get there!

Once they reach the mountain, they'd rather carry everything on their backs than distribute it among some porters who live on what they earn from their work. But don't these people go to the store in a car? Don't they take an elevator once they get home? Do they light their nightstand with candles?

I'd been hearing about these people for a while, and I'd even read about them. From time to time I'd run into one of them, but it's difficult to tell them apart from everyone else since they blend into the rest of society well. Your physics or philosophy teacher might belong to this clan without you knowing. Or that computer programmer who uses strange words to talk about his job, or the supermarket cashier who scans the barcodes, or the guy who stops you in the street when there's construction going on. You won't know who they are until you see them refuse the amenities available on the mountain.

On that trip to Nepal in 2012, I got involved with two members of this cult without fully realizing until it was too late: Jordi Tosas and Jordi Corominas. And ever since then, I've been part of that band of loonies. I noticed the first symptoms of my abduction when I caught myself uttering the words of the gurus in this sect—words like "We shouldn't adapt the mountains to our needs but work on our abilities to adapt ourselves to the mountains." Now that I think of it, maybe going against evolution is the perfect way to evolve.

SOME YEARS LATER, IN 2017, WHEN WINTER WAS ALMOST OVER, I was set to return in a few weeks to the Himalayas. Since that previous summer, I'd been thinking about the areas I needed to improve to be more efficient and, as Jordi Tosas put it, to become a sniper. The first change I needed to make had to do with the upcoming trip. It was essential for it to be short, so as not to waste my energy or motivation on travel, and to achieve this, I had to work hard on the logistics. The China Tibet Mountaineering Association, which grants mountain-climbing permits, and the other agencies involved in the trip all needed to understand that tourism wasn't my goal. I didn't want to visit Kathmandu and make little stops along the way, visiting landmarks and slowly acclimating. What I wanted was to get to the mountains as fast as possible because I would be already acclimated.

Acclimation was the second point I needed to work on. Based on my experiences in previous years, I had designed a protocol that consisted of my spending three hundred hours at a high altitude before the climb, either training or sleeping. The training was very intense, since in the morning I went out to the mountains near my home on the Norwegian west coast on skis from four to ten, then in the afternoon I ran intensely at a high altitude for an hour. After this, I was so beat that the dizziness lasted a couple of hours. The morning training prepared me physically and also mentally, with the goal of feeling comfortable on the mountain. The great difficulty of high mountains is not feeling good because the conditions are so different from day-to-day life. I had to prepare my body and mind to feel a certain level of comfort in situations that might arise. This is what we usually call *accepting compromise*, which just means coming to terms with the uncertainty of what might happen.

When you're in an uncertain situation, you need to be able to control your emotions, even find a way to eliminate them, and let reason and instinct lead your actions.

MY HEART WAS BEATING HARDER. *PUM-PUM, PUM-PUM*. NOT FASTER, but with greater intensity. Each stroke made me tremble, as if reminding me I was alive, that my heart was there, working to keep me in the world. My legs wanted to move forward, but I didn't know what was happening; something was preventing them, slowing their pace, maybe waiting for a sign that could be translated into an excuse to turn around and go back to flatter terrain.

I felt fear and desire at the same time. I slowed my pace, inspecting the wall up ahead, examining every centimeter so precisely that I felt my hands sweat inside my gloves, as if they were already gripping the ice axes. I would have paid money to have already begun to climb, but at the same time, navigating that unknown ocean in the shape of an icy stone wall was what I feared most. For days, I had fantasized, imagining my body as it climbed. I was fully motivated, and there was nothing I wanted more than to be *doing* it. But paradoxically, instead of accelerating, my pace had slowed down. My senses, highly concentrated, searched for the tiniest signal, seeking a final excuse to quit with a clear conscience, convinced that this wasn't a defeat but rather a victory for experience and good judgment.

With my brain a battleground between rational and emotional urges, I gradually approached the wall. I stopped for a moment at its base, where a small crevasse opened beneath me. It was time to make *the* final decision. Which of the warring sides would win? My instinct for comfort or my acceptance of compromise?

I drove the two ice axes in and began to climb.

Though I hadn't reached the point of no return, since I could still retrace the meters I had climbed, I knew there was only one possible direction: straight ahead and up.

The ice slope became progressively vertical, and I climbed at a constant, melodic pace, fluid and calm. A first vertical section took me to a short, more comfortable area where I could rest my forearms, which were beginning to accumulate lactic acid. As I stretched my arms to relax them, I looked down: about 80 meters away I could make out my footprints in the snow, zigzagging until they reached the wall; farther down, the thread diminished and disappeared at the end of the valley.

I climbed a few more meters of easy terrain until the next vertical section, about 20 meters of ice, only a few centimeters thick and covering smooth rock. I drove in an ice axe and saw that the pick went in easily. Too easily. The hard, solid ice I had found until then had become a slush of frozen snow that stuck to the rock. I put my weight on the ice axe and slipped, dragging the slush down. *God damn it!*

I HAD FALLEN IN LOVE WITH THIS WALL A FEW DAYS AFTER EMELIE and I arrived in Romsdal. It wasn't as high as the neighboring Trollveggen, or as beautiful as Romsdalshorn. I saw it every time I went to town, distant and close at the same time. I hadn't found a single book that talked about it, or any map or route, and this made it all the more attractive. It was a 600-meter stone wall facing north, eternally in shadow. From the town, you could see its shape, vertical black granite, with thin waterfalls of ice that appeared and disappeared in the middle of the wall, and an ice *goulotte*, or chute, that went down diagonally from one of the sides but was abruptly left hanging about 100 meters from the ground, which meant that to reach it you had to climb those 100 meters of smooth rock. It was extremely vertical, impossible to climb without gear. However, luck had sent a wind from the north, bringing snow that fell not vertically but sideways, and with the humidity from the sea, the snow and ice had stayed literally stuck to the wall. This was a gift, and now I had a chance to reach the *goulotte* I saw every day.

When I reached that point, I realized the ice was thick enough to support my weight on vertical terrain. Doubt took hold of my entire being; that day my brain told me I was going to climb the wall, but once I was there . . . I still had the option of carefully climbing down the 80 meters I'd climbed up and skiing back home, or climbing another nearby mountain to let off steam. But no. I tried the assault again, looking for a weak spot in the waterfall. First I approached it from the right, but the ice didn't get any thicker. I went down a few meters until I found solid ice and took the opportunity to stretch my arms. The *goulotte* was only about 20 meters away, and before going down I tried one last time to the left. I'd wanted to avoid that side of the waterfall because it was at the edge of the rock, which was made up of completely smooth, vertical sheets, and I could see that the ice was no thicker than 10 centimeters. *Here we go—fantastic!* As I drove the first ice axe in, I felt some ice a little more solid than what was in the middle of the waterfall. Here at least it supported weight, but since it was so thin, I couldn't plunge the ice axe in hard; that could crack the thick part of the ice. I drove it in gently, until one or two teeth sunk in, then I lifted my foot, barely touching the ice, and used an opening of rock to rest the tip of my crampon. Holding my breath, I climbed the 20 vertical meters quickly until the ice thickened again. A couple of meters slightly collapsed from ice accumulation forced me to drive the ice axes in hard and not look down into the 100-meter void there must have been between my legs. I clung so hard to the ice axes that if one of my hands or feet gave way, I was sure I'd still be able to hold on.

When I reached the beginning of the *goulotte*, I took a deep breath and let out all my fear and adrenaline. The difficulties seemed less pronounced, or at least weren't as constant, but from then on, the only way out was up. If I came upon some insurmountable difficulty, I wouldn't be able to climb back down. I kept climbing, finding obstacles at every step and deciding where to keep going, trusting blindly in my intuition.

I know perfectly well that many people think the line between total commitment and thoughtlessness is very thin, if indeed they think there is a line at all. The most plausible result of a fall from a great height is death, and any exception would come down to extraordinary luck. But what lies behind an accepted commitment, even in unfamiliar terrain, is the result of a careful study of conditions and painstaking planning, after scrutinizing the difficulties over and over, from the foot of a wall or from other peaks.

You must have the risks implied by a technical climb ingrained in your mind, and know that you're good enough to overcome them. A climb can be easy, moderate, comfortable, or extremely difficult, and based on this, you accept or reject the challenge. If you fall, it will be because you overestimated your technical skill or made a mistake, including in choosing your equipment.

You also have to be careful about the dangers the mountain itself presents: the risk of avalanches, the ice quality or loose rock, the weather—many factors can intervene. But no matter how committed you are, you always have to accept that there's an element of chance, and that you can't always be in control.

You have to muster a thousand resources to be able to make a quick decision, and the right one if it happens to be necessary.

The perception of risk is a personal matter. While it's true that it depends on an equation involving individual ability and experience, and the conditions and difficulties of the mountain in question, committing to a climb is always a personal choice.

I CAME TO THE LAST STRETCH OF ROCK AND GLIMPSED THE LEDGE that had formed on the ridge, climbed those meters calmly, reached the top of the wall and the summit, then went down the other side.

Since it was still early and I had the whole day ahead of me, I climbed up to another peak, and another, and then another, until the horizon began to slice through the sun. Finally, I decided to go home, satisfied to have conquered my fears that day.

Experiences That Changed Me Forever

We were searching for shade under large tropical trees. The heat had turned the mighty riverbed into an oven. We had reached a wide beach, at a point where the deep canyon widened a little, allowing the sun to filter in through the thick jungle. The sun burned our skin, but a gentle breeze lifted the stifling, sultry air. We were covered in dust and mud.

We'd been waiting all day for the helicopter that would take us back to Kathmandu. We'd taken the heaviest stones from the beach and used them to mark a flat area where the helicopter could land. The silence of the sky, though, was absolute. We had to move the heavy body a couple of times. Though we had wrapped it in plastic bags, when the sun bore down on it, the smell was unbearable.

The day before, we had carried the remains of that anonymous man down paths buried by rockslides, until we found the beach. You wouldn't believe how heavy a corpse can be. On the most technical stretches, we'd needed five or six people. And without really knowing how, we were sharing what little food we had left with half a dozen guys from Tzahal, the Israel Defense Forces. We didn't talk much since obviously the atmosphere was kind of weird.

They had come to search for their friend, hoping he'd survived the earthquake that shook Nepal that spring in 2015, and we had just spent a week getting our backpacks ready to try to climb Everest as part of the Summits of My Life project. It was an odd mixture: three committed pacifists and six soldiers from the Gaza border. The exhaustion was starting to show. They hadn't been able to find their friend alive, but they were determined to bury him in his home country. For our part, we weren't sure why we'd agreed to help with this expensive and pointless enterprise, to recover a body from a valley where three hundred more were buried beneath the rubble.

In the last few days as we climbed through the valley, we had found dozens of dead bodies, which we reported via satellite to the Kathmandu embassies and the military units of different countries that had dared to deploy to the area. The earthquake had been a true catastrophe for Nepal, where houses are little more than dry stone shelters that collapse with the slightest shake.

What destiny awaited the rest of the bodies scattered throughout the valley? It was horrifying to witness the abyss between the resources invested in recovering a rich foreign tourist's body and the oblivion to which Nepalese children and elderly people who shared his misfortune beneath the tons of rock were condemned.

International aid for the earthquake's victims was massive.

Nepal is poor but each year welcomes a million tourists from wealthy countries, which explains the immense resources deployed to try to return the country to normality. Yet despite the high number of groups of all kinds present on the ground, the coordination was appalling, and on top of that, the government pocketed as many of the donations it received as it could. And a great deal of energy was spent on bureaucracy.

The help we offered was negligible, but for Séb Montaz, Jordi Tosas, and me, the experience was branded into our memories. We worked for a month, helping first with the military to search for and identify the dead in the Langtang Valley, and then helping various NGOs take food to survivors and assess the damage in the highest, least accessible villages of the Ganesh region, which we could reach only by running and after a few days' journey. By the end, we were exhausted.

ON MY RETURN, I MADE AN EFFORT TO GET BACK TO MY NORMAL LIFE as quickly as possible, where my concerns were barely more serious than being more or less in shape, having the logistics in place to run a race, and deciding if the news on the radio was of any interest. For a brief period, we had experienced a serious, concrete reality in which the big headaches were real: eat, sleep, survive to save the lives of others. After leaving all that behind, I decided to turn a new page and change my flight to go straight to Zegama, where I would run a marathon the next day.

From the beginning of the race, I felt good. The fact that I'd just spent a month at high altitude gave me strength. But despite that, my head was somewhere else while I ran surrounded by thousands of spectators, and I felt dirty for taking center stage in a trivial, unproductive activity, and for being immersed in the euphoria that comes from the spectacle of runners and fans. Somewhere else, just a short plane ride away, life was very different.

We live in a world of parallel realities that observe but choose not to understand each other. When we get up in the morning and browse the news or check Twitter, we get the false impression that we are everywhere. We see images of a terrorist attack in Baghdad, a protest in Murcia, or a migrant boat that's just sunk off the coast of Greece . . . and since we are all parents, children, or immigrants, we identify with what's going on. A few seconds later, we read a comment by a politician out of context, and we either applaud or get mad. Then a viral video grabs our attention, and we laugh our heads off at something dumb. And then . . . and then . . . Everything seems close. We experience everything virtually. It's easy to get updated on everything, every day. Until the moment you find an article about something you know a lot about, and you feel a pit in your stomach as you read, because you're suddenly amazed to realize what kind of drivel people write. And in the end, this makes you doubt the truth of any news from an area you're unfamiliar with. Appearances end up prevailing over facts, and the issue is often reduced to finding an easy polemic to draw people into the media. Meanwhile, injustice continues, far from any debate, and those who suffer keep suffering in their world. You can wear your fingers out clicking on LIKE and sharing links: the two parallel realities will never converge.

For a few years now in our society, our materialistic focus on personal image has become as important as our capitalist, materialistic focus on well-being. Until recently, the cultivation of a personal image was limited to politicians and pop stars, but today, nobody is immune. It all began when they started trying to put us at the center of everything, with the typical entrepreneurial slogans, like "You are your own brand!" It continued with companies choosing potential employees based on their social-networking profiles. Or with tech multinationals deciding whether we were better or worse, authentic and unique or a waste of space, according to how many comments or likes we received. Or with our loss of privacy, when it became possible for anyone who cared to find out what you ate, what music you listened to, where you bought your socks, who you admired, and where you were thinking of going on your next vacation. We've become obsessed, and now we're like putty, working away at trying to fit into a mold. We have ended up turning into—they have turned us into—a tiny piece of the commercial world.

It's becoming harder and harder to see the line between what we call "I" and what we say is "mine." We have come to believe that we "are" what we "have": my body, my mental faculties, my clothes, my house, my husband or wife, my children and friends, and even my reputation, work, and bank account. We base our feelings on what we have, and lose sight of our interest in what we are. The rules of satisfaction or frustration depend on whether we can attach a possessive adjective to a noun. And this trend seems very difficult to change.

Sports have not been immune to the shift. In fact, they've been subjected to it faster and more intensely than other spheres. The sports we are sold today are a spectacle, and a spectacle needs an audience. And the audiences are no longer in the stadiums. Or, to put it another way: yes, they are—they're in the one massive stadium the world has become. Everyone has a preferred seat, in their home. An athlete is an athlete twenty-four hours a day and, on top of training, he has to live "authentically" and have a "take" on everything. And since he's no longer just talking to four freaks who understand him—the audience is no longer a minority but global—everything he says must be straightforward and simplified, to quickly catch the attention of a public that consumes information at the speed of a machine gun firing a round of bullets. I know I have five or six seconds to produce a spectacular image that will leave you, the spectator, breathless, and grab your attention because it's interesting and not just entertaining. There's no need for complicated explanations and "insignificant" details, since those can get a little too interesting. You have to go straight for an easy headline, for a number that's easy to understand and compare, for competition between news items, athletes, people.

We do it to "reach" people, but then we realize that by trying to reach everyone else, there's one detail we've neglected: we can no longer reach ourselves. And we have changed our perspective without fully realizing it, because we act, think, and write with the knowledge that we're being watched and analyzed by an audience. As a result, we are changing what we do, and especially how we do it.

I WASN'T COMPLETELY IMMUNE TO THIS. PEOPLE WANTED ME TO WIN more races, and since it was pretty easy for me, I did, but then they expected me to break records by conquering such-and-such peak or climbing such-and-such mountain, or to say something appropriate, or to defend what I should supposedly be defending. While for a long time what I wanted and what people asked of me were one and the same, now, without my knowing very well how, the bond was broken and I was a prisoner of other people's projects.

When I came back from Nepal in 2015, from that devastated inferno where Western opulence contrasts with local poverty, I felt the hypocrisy of parallel worlds in an intense and personal way, and I was convinced that, without my wanting it, everything could come crashing to an end in the blink of an eye. And I didn't want the fateful day to come when I had to face what I hadn't done while waiting for a future that might not exist. I didn't want my career to change course even a bit, just so I could win more races, fame, or money. And even if this decision forced me to destroy the image I'd created of myself, I wanted to kill Kilian Jornet, to kill the "personality."

SEMANTICS ARE IMPORTANT. OUR NAME ACCUMULATES CONNOTATIONS, and as the years go by, it stops being simply what people call us and becomes a backpack loaded with things we can no longer shed. If we can't understand and dominate our surroundings, we get anxious, so we name everything to create the illusion that we understand it, and that it belongs to us. If a place has no name, it doesn't exist. Language is the vehicle for our thoughts, and if we don't find the exact word to describe what we think, see, or feel, everything is lost to oblivion and disappears, has never "existed."

We know philosophical movements by what they're called; people have names, and mountains, too. The people of Grindelwald didn't call the mountain in whose shadow they lived Eiger ("ogre") just for the sake of it; the same goes for the Italians, who named the Aosta Valley pyramid Cervino (which alludes to the Italian word for red deer, *cervo,* abundant in the area), and the Swiss on the other side, who called it Matterhorn (the "peak in the meadows"). Names can be logical and descriptive, like Mont Blanc—the "white mountain"—or Pedraforca, named for the forked shape of its rocky peak. We also have Puro, the Pic du Midi . . . Sometimes, the imagination runs wild and sees human attributes in nature: Grand Teton in Wyoming—for the breast-like shape of the peaks—or the Cavall Bernat in Montserrat, where the *cavall* is an adaptation of the Catalan word *carall*, meaning "penis." Or Shivling in the Himalayas—the penis again, with its connection to the Sanskrit *lingum.* Other names come from beliefs that mountains have almost supernatural characteristics, like Mont Maudit—haunted—the Aiguilles du Diable, the Pic de l'Infern, or Monte Disgrazia. In some cases it's not exactly the imagination that's in charge, and a series of letters and numbers refer to a mountain in a country the topographer doesn't know, as is the case of K1 and K2. There are also mountains named for their "discoverer," not taking into account that the inhabitants of the place in question must have already had a name for it: Mount McKinley, Mont Cook, Monte Fitz Roy, Pico Russell. Everest, the highest of all, belongs to this category. During the years of the British Empire, the colonizers made maps of India and called it Peak XV, but when they realized it was the highest peak of all, they baptized it in honor of George Everest, the chief surveyor. It didn't matter that the Tibetans had been calling it Qomolangma for over three hundred years. The Nepalese, when they saw it attracted tourists, contributed to its abundance of names, calling it Sagarmatha.

The strength of the word inspires fear, since its meaning can change according to how it's pronounced. It can calm or terrorize, trivialize or glorify. But it's important to understand that the mountains' existence precedes the names people have given them. Whatever they're called, they will keep being themselves, just as people will still exist if we have no first or last name; we still have feelings, even if we cannot find words to describe them.

My heart, I realized at the time, was telling me I wanted to return to climbing unnamed mountains, so that I might feel again, without knowing how to describe my feelings.

TWO YEARS HAD GONE BY SINCE THE NEPALESE EARTHQUAKE, AND I was in Norway, at the farm where I live with Emelie. We were reinforcing a fence that we'd built not long before. The previous week we had noticed the sheep could jump the wire fence, and once they discovered this ability, they wasted no time at all, imitating the star of *The Great Escape* whenever they could. Until one of them got stuck. It had to learn, through a painful experience, the nature of the traps you can fall into when looking for freedom.

We didn't know how long their new respect for the fence would last, or when they would recover the will to flee and start jumping higher, so we wanted to preempt them and decided to increase the height in some parts. That morning I had to go to town and decided to buy the posts and the length of wire we needed so I could finish the job that afternoon. When I asked for the materials at the store, the sales assistant immediately noticed that my Norwegian accent wasn't exactly orthodox. As he helped me load my purchase into the car, he told me in perfect English and with a smile almost too big for his face that he was glad for-eigners enjoyed living in these dead-end mountains. He asked me if I was from Morocco. I said yes, more or less around there.

We finished the fence in the end, though I'm not much of a handyman. I'm not a big fan of chaining myself to a single place, but it's nice to see your work bear fruit. Suddenly, I felt like I owed all the time I spent away from home climbing mountains to Emelie.

AT THAT TIME OF YEAR, IN EARLY SUMMER, THE SUN NEVER GOES down, and it's a good time to go running for hours on end. Running is pure, simple, and human. The closest to it is walking, which is just what runners do when they're tired. Both activities fulfill one of human beings' most basic goals: to move around. For me, this is a basic drive of life. Without it, there's no way to learn. And what's more, once you set out in a direction, you can branch out and multiply it infinitely.

Every day of the year, I go out running or skiing to train, but there's a fundamental difference between training and com-pleting an expedition: the uncertainty of whether you'll achieve what you set out to do. And after a year out of action due to in-juries, I now wanted to do something to challenge myself, to live intensely again, to find my limit in some concrete aspect of what I do. The idea of a long journey didn't appeal to me. *Beauty is often hiding right outside your door*, I thought. That's why I de-cided on a simple but highly demanding expedition: leave the house, climb a mountain, and follow the ridge of the summits until my legs and heart tell me they've had enough, that they cannot go on.

One Friday in late July, I filled my backpack with everything I might need for a few days in the mountains, constantly on the go: a jacket, some gloves, about twenty energy bars, a short rope, an ice axe, and not much else. After breakfast, I went out running as I do every day, except this time I didn't know when I'd be coming home. Emelie went with me as far as the first peak, in the midst of a fog that tinted the valleys a sad shade of gray. After 1,000 meters, we reached the top and had a great time running as if on top of a sea of cotton wool, our faces warmed by the sun and our eyes making out the sharp islands that rose up along the horizon. *I want to stay here, running from peak to peak along the ridges that join them, and never enter the clouds.* Emelie and I said goodbye. She turned back, and I kept going along the top of the ridge, doing a balancing act so as not to be swallowed up by the surrounding clouds. They were white and soft, but they wouldn't have cushioned my fall.

Normally when I set out on an expedition my first move is to set my stopwatch. This time, I didn't. Speed is embedded in my DNA, but I didn't want to rush; rather, I wanted to go far and not leave a record.

Step by step, stone by stone, peak by peak, I followed the ridge. The sun's heat grew stronger and I was alone on top of the clouds. Everyone else was inside the fog, lamenting the gray, and didn't know they had this paradise so close—if only they'd come up here for a while. That idyllic place unfurled before my eyes like a snake. A dozen peaks, one after another, connected by a narrow strip of rock; a little beyond lay another dozen, and then another, though they were so far away that I couldn't make them out clearly. But I was getting closer, dancing a fluid dance, flirting with a little danger to make it more exciting. I played around with difficulties not outside my comfort zone, but they did require an effort for me to stay safe. I was exploring the creation of a private, intimate moment.

I didn't know what time it was, and my body couldn't be tricked by the illusion that time didn't matter. I'd been gaining elevation for over 7,000 meters by now, and the tiredness was beginning to show. The ridge I'd been following all day came to an end, and I had to go down to the valley to climb into the adjoining range and start a new ridge. I left the rocks and the snow behind for a forested area that grew thicker and thicker, until I could distinguish the smell of the sea and spot the first houses in a town. At that latitude, the summer sun goes down for a couple of hours, and it was exactly that time, with a dark dot on the horizon, when I crossed the still-sleeping town. So as not to disturb anyone, I tiptoed in front of the houses and went on across to the other side of the valley, leaving behind the smell of the sea and the thick trees and bushes until I reached the area where I feel most comfortable, the mineral world.

The shadows persisted when I attacked the next ridge; a narrow, vertical edge showed me where to begin. About 400 meters of reddish wall challenged me, and as I approached, I tried with little success to identify its weak spot. When I reached the foot of the wall, I saw a system of cracks and dihedrals that looked continuous, and I began to climb. It was a grade V level of difficulty. Though it wasn't demanding, it required a vertical dance of concentration and precise movements. My sneakers stuck softly to the granite, and my fingers moved delicately across the cracks so as not to disturb them. On this kind of terrain, where the rock barely sees any people, and even more so when you climb without the backup of a rope, you have to caress more than cling. Before grasping or stepping onto my target, I would tap it gently with my hand or foot, to make sure it was firm enough to resist my weight. With each step, as I danced with the rock in a vertical position, I asked its permission to take it by the waist, knowing that the slightest false step would cause me to fall and break my heart.

When I reached the upper section, the wall became less vertical and therefore less solid.

Between the cracks, which grew wider and more frequent, a few clumps of grass were growing, practically the only mortar that kept the rocks stuck to the wall. At some points I even took out my ice axe and drove it into a thicket to achieve a safe enough degree of stability. Slowly but surely, I overcame these obstacles and reached the ridges again. Since I was now back in a less risky stretch, my body spoke and told me it was getting very, very tired. Despite my strategy of eating a bar or gel every couple of hours, it must have been over twenty hours since I began running and climbing, without stopping for even a second. A blanket of exhaustion fell over me like the night, covering me completely.

There was nothing I could do. No matter how much I ate, the energy didn't return to my feet. Even with the fresh memory of my light steps, they couldn't run, and I had to drag them across the rocks. The landscape didn't advance, and between one peak and another, time seemed to go on forever.

It's moments like this when you ask yourself what the point is of going on. My body ached and was falling asleep, my movements were clumsy, and every step took so much concentration on the more technical stretches that my pace slowed to half of what it had been. My head was fighting fatigue, waiting for a nice spot to fall down on the grass, bask in the sun, take a nap, and breathe for a few minutes. But that was impossible. It was still a few hours until the sunlight would bathe that face of the mountain, and first I wanted to get through the more technical stretch. The ridge I had to traverse was made up of a dozen pinnacles of various shapes and sizes, some so narrow that a group of four people could embrace them, others with a perimeter of over half a kilometer, and a few hundred meters high.

In the middle of my battle with sleep and my feet's protest, pushed along by a force of stubbornness, I reached the final peak on the ridge. I looked up for a moment and contemplated the wall that fell away beneath me: a sheer 1,500-meter drop to the river on which it stood. If I threw a rock down here, it would plunge into the water without even grazing the wall.

I approached the edge of the ridge and unrolled the rope. I was looking for a block of stone solid enough to resist my weight. I found it and slid the cord down behind me. Since it was very thin, I could retrieve it from below after rappelling, without needing to leave any gear on the wall. I set up three rappels, climbed down a little, and reached a glacier, which allowed me to slide down and save some energy. I was soon at the bottom of the valley. A road led me to Åndalsnes, a town of two thousand inhabitants. Seeing so many people so suddenly made me realize I'd been running for a little more than a day without encountering anyone.

I took the chance to buy some energy bars at a gas station. A slice of bread and cheese and a half-hour nap gave me back the vitality I'd had when I set out. I kept going and went up to the next ridge, and, running and climbing, I mounted its peaks. This was a more touristy area, and from time to time I came across people admiring the view or climbers tackling a wall. Their company livened up the route. I used them to spur myself on: *See if you can get to the summit before the guy in the red jacket. You'll catch up with that rope team before they finish their meeting.* Just a childish game to keep myself awake.

With this formula, I managed to trick my exhaustion until a few hours later, when it took hold of my entire body. My feet were heavy and refused to obey my brain's instructions. It was late afternoon, and there were still four hours of sun left. The challenge ahead of me was the highest peak in the region. It had a long descent, and I wanted to reach it before the shadows, so the snow would still be softened by the heat of the day and I could go down faster and more safely. A few hours later, hidden in darkness, it would be as hard as glass.

The ridge I was facing wasn't difficult, but it was involved and exposed, and required a certain amount of concentration. In the state I was in, it might take me three or four hours to reach the top safely. I was so sleepy! My vision was even blurry when I looked at the path. When you feel like you're falling asleep when you're walking along, you feel so anxious. And when I saw a little patch of grass between some rocks, it looked so good. A deep happiness overcame me when I imagined lying there with my eyes closed, sleeping like a baby. Few things can compete with a sense of well-being like that one. I took off my shoes and socks and left them in the sun to dry, rolled my jacket into the shape of a cushion, set the alarm on my phone to go off half an hour later, and stretched out on the soft grass. Then I was knocked out by sleep.

I was sleeping deeply when a buzzing sound awoke me. *The time!* The sun was still caressing my face, the heat was as pleasant as the gentle breeze blowing away the stifling warmth.

Almost robotically, I pulled on my shoes and socks and set out again as if nothing had happened. After a minute back on my way, my body was awake enough and I began to jog, and I didn't stop running until I had reached the first wall of rock. My hands set about their task easily and my feet corresponded with lightness, and with the precision I had lost a few hours earlier. The ridge went by beneath my feet at a speed I would have been satisfied with on a shorter run, and I experienced it with a feeling closer to happiness than excitement, the feeling you get when your body and spirit align. It was hard to believe I'd been having such a hard time just an hour before, struggling to stay awake, punishing myself by wondering why I didn't just give up and go home. And look, soon after that, here I was, galloping along as if I'd only just gotten up, with a joy I wouldn't have traded for anything in the world. I knew that feeling, that illusion of freshness, would soon give way to another, and I wanted to experience it as intensely as possible.

It took me only an hour to reach the summit, and I let myself slide down the soft snow as the sun went down. Halfway along the ridge, I swung over to the darker side, abandoning the warmth and at the same time the more traveled area, sure it would be about twenty hours before I saw anyone again.

Among lakes and waterfalls, with no scarcity of water, the ridges were once again painted a shade of black that covered the fractured rocks of dubious solidity, and my body's freshness disappeared just like the sun. I was wiped out all over again. With extreme fatigue, we take more risks due to laziness and exhaustion. Once it had been forty hours since I'd left home, I spent my energy trying not to fall into the traps set by my mind, and to prevent the lazy Kilian from beating the rational Kilian. To prevent monotony from teaming up with exhaustion, I tried hard to remember the lyrics of an Italian song that I repeated over and over on a loop: *"Ma ho visto anche degli zingari felici, corrersi dietro, far l'amore e rotolarsi per terra. Ho visto anche degli zingari felici . . . Zingari . . ."*

The sun rose over the horizon again and I awaited its warmth. A sea of clouds enveloped the highest peaks once more. On my way down, I passed a stream and stopped to wash my face, which was covered in days of sweat. The cool water revived me. I drank so much that it unsettled my stomach. I walked a little farther away from the edge of the river and stretched out in a grassy dip. The sun's heat accompanied me while I slept.

Somewhat recovered and climbing the next ridge, I counted the remaining peaks on my fingers. My whole hand, five fingers, and I would finish circling the fjord along the ridges! If you'd told me I'd make it this far thirty hours earlier when I was sunk in a pit of exhaustion, I wouldn't have believed it. And now! Five peaks didn't seem like many, but after 160 kilometers and more than 20,000 meters of uphill slope in fifty hours, I couldn't lose my respect for the more than 4,000 still ahead. So, with my batteries recharged after a half-hour nap and the carrot of rest—this time definitive—dangling in front of my nose, I shot off at full speed along those rocky hills.

Maybe it was because of the excitement of glimpsing the end, or maybe the exhaustion, that I forgot the caution mantra I'd been repeating for so many hours. Wanting to take the middle of the path, without paying much attention to where I was putting my feet, I fell to the bottom of a small crevasse just as I was crossing the last stretch of snow. It was very soft. I sunk up to above my knees, tempting fate a little too much by trusting blindly in the solidity of its bridges of snow, until one of them gave way beneath my feet. The hole wasn't very deep, a couple of meters at the most, but my hip impacted directly against the slick gray rock. A sharp pain shot up my spine. I sat down to breathe deeply for a few seconds and soothe the pain. I confirmed that nothing serious had happened. Everything was still in working order, and the lump about to appear on my hip was a foregone conclusion, so I set off back into the snow. I looked for a path among the stones, like I should have from the beginning. "This is just superficial damage," I said. And I started running.

I soon forgot the pain, and the promise of reaching the end was a balm that gave me energy. Three peaks, two peaks, and finally I began to climb the narrow ridge that led to the fjord's last summit. I had laid my exhaustion and desire to rest in some corner, I'm not sure where. Among the clouds, in the distance, in the middle of the ridge, Emelie appeared. She was waiting for me with a kiss and a sandwich in her hand. She accompanied me to the last peak, and we went down to the town together. I sat for a few minutes in the trunk of the car, not eating or drinking, not taking off my clothes, which by this time were a second skin. I stared vacantly at some point on the road. My mind was blank. This absence is probably where all the force of our activities resides. When you finish them, for a brief period, there is no past or future.

IT WAS A STUPID THING TO DO, JUST THREE MONTHS AFTER BREAKING my fibula in the Pierra Menta. I'm sure no doctor would have recommended it as part of my rehab, and mine never found out about it. Until now, I guess. But these are exactly the things I live for: exploring in the knowledge that the risk of failure is high. As well as testing how my recovery was going, what most interested me was to combine two activities I excelled at: long-distance running—160 or 200 kilometers are no challenge for me—and climbing, in which I didn't know how I would respond to doing so many walls, one right after another. In the end, I know that to achieve intense enjoyment, I have to go to the limit of my comfort zone, then stick to the range of things I know how to do, stretching the limit as far as possible.

EVEREST IN
SPRING

A few weeks after leaving the Norwegian winter behind, I returned to the same powder-and-rock esplanade of the previous summer, Everest. Now everything was different.

The moraine where we had embraced eight months ago was covered in tents of every shape, size, and color a creative mind could imagine. The ridge we had descended between avalanches was now a placid and gentle slope of hardened snow, with a cord attached to some stakes that ran from where the snow began all the way to the mountain's summit. Some three hundred people were walking between Rongbuk and the last camp, situated at 8,300 meters, half of them harboring a dream of reaching the summit, the other half working so that those in the first group could achieve their goal. Last year's solitary camp had become a small multicultural city, where everyone was absorbed in the work of preparing for the ascent.

Séb and I were sharing a permit with another expedition that had already been set up on the mountain for a few weeks. I was coming from a neighboring expedition on Cho Oyu, where I had spent a week with Emelie. Séb had just arrived from France. Even though he'd been at a high altitude for the last few weeks in Tibet and then in the Alps, he'd had a terrible night. He had a dry cough and chest pain, and spit a little blood when he coughed. It was a sign of a pulmonary edema. We'd have to take it easy and wait a few days before going up to the advanced base camp.

That first day, we visited the members of the expedition sharing our permit. One of them was a doctor, but not a specialist in mountaineering. He took one look at Séb and his symptoms and said gravely: "You have something really serious. A pulmonary edema is no joke. You have to go down right away! Take the medicine I'm going to give you, if you wake up tomorrow—"

Before the well-intentioned doctor could finish his sentence, Séb and I burst out laughing like a pair of mischievous boys. We already knew what was going on, and while it was a nuisance, it posed no great risk. A couple of days of rest, and he'd be good to go. At most, he might have to return to the foothills for a day to recuperate. In fact, the same thing had happened a few years ago when we went to Mount Elbrus, but as soon as he went down to a lower altitude, he recovered.

Séb had a rough night, but the next day he was feeling better. He spent one more day recovering. On the third day, when he got up, he was able to run around the camp area, so we decided to go up to the advanced base camp at the foot of the mountain, where the yaks hadn't wanted to go last year.

Once we'd set up camp, I went out to train and acclimate, and to check out the conditions on the mountain. Since the idea of attempting an ascent via the northeast face, where we'd left off a year ago, was still on my mind, I set off in the opposite direction of everyone else. I strayed from the track that led to the northern pass and crossed the glacier until I reached the foot of the north wall. There was far less snow than in summer. *Fewer avalanches!* This also meant there was much more ice.

I started to climb. The ice beneath me felt rock hard; the 10 centimeters of snow that covered it merely whitened it but added no firmness, and I supported my whole body weight on what little of my crampons and ice axe I could drive in. Since it wasn't too steep, I started climbing anyway, until I'd made it a few hundred meters. Suddenly I stopped and asked myself what I was doing there. *Aren't you taking too many risks?* If I'd faced these conditions last year, I was sure I would have kept climbing without thinking twice, but now, the truth was I was not feeling very at ease. What had happened a week ago had made me lower the threshold of risks I was willing to take.

IT HAD BEEN A WEEK SINCE I WAS ON CHO OYU WITH EMELIE. OUR acclimation and training in Norway had gone perfectly, and then—after a battle with the Nepalese bureaucracy, as despair-inducing as it was routine—we made a quick journey that got us to base camp in only three days, feeling refreshed and motivated.

My second day on the mountain, I received one of those messages that are hard to read. That morning, we had climbed from the camp to over 6,000 meters, and we were doing surprisingly well. When we came down, the smiles on our faces didn't last long. I turned on my satellite phone to check the weather conditions and started to tidy the tent while the phone searched for coverage. After a few minutes, I heard the beep that indicated a message. Only two people have that phone number: Emelie, who was by my side, and Jordi Lorenzo, my agent. I used it just once a week to tell him I was fine so he could pass the news on to my family. If there was a message, something important must have happened. I picked up the phone and unlocked the screen.

"Have you heard what happened to Ueli? He died on Nuptse."

Everything clouded over. An entire value system collapses each time one of the pillars sustaining it dies on the mountain. And all the questions arise again. "Is it right to do what we do?" "What's the point of all the risks we take to climb a mountain?" "Up to what point is the pleasure of an activity more important than what we risk losing?"

I know that when I'm up there, I'm not looking for death but life. Yet sometimes it's harder to understand. Then I thought of Nicole, Ueli Steck's wife, and also of Emelie, who was reading beside me and still didn't know what had happened.

UP THERE ON THE MOUNTAIN IS WHERE I FIND RELIEF FROM PAIN. Death, for me, would be to not go at all.

The day after getting the painful news, we went up again. We were walking at a good pace and reached 7,500 meters fairly quickly. We were in good physical shape, and this showed that our acclimation had been successful, since it had been only eight days since we had left Europe.

We'd been noticing for a while that bad weather was on its way, and decided to go down and wait for the next window of good conditions to try to reach the summit. That year in the spring there were only a couple of commercial expeditions, and since nobody seemed too keen to get up the mountain—fix the ropes and set up the camp for clients—we found that we had it all to ourselves.

I told Emelie to start going down while I took a look at where we would need to get past the yellow band on our next attempt. This is a fairly steep strip of rock of about 50 meters, characterized by its yellow color, which can be seen in all mountains in the Himalayas, at an altitude of between 7,800 and 8,200 meters. I climbed a dozen meters to get a better look. Once I had looked and looked again, I turned back to see if Emelie was getting down without any trouble. *Shit!* My heart stopped and I was speechless when I saw her sliding down the snow at high speed, upside down on her stomach. She was falling uncontrollably down a forty-degree slope covered in hard snow that led to . . . Well, it was better not to think about it, if she didn't manage to break her fall. As soon as I got my voice back I began to shout, and went down as fast as I could, following the tracks her ice axes had left in the snow as she tried to hold on. I reached the point where Emelie had lost the first one. "Stop! Please, stop!" I couldn't breathe and my heart had stopped pumping blood. Finally, about 100 meters farther down, she managed to break her fall with the one she had left. When I reached her, my heart started beating again, this time fast and out of control. I hugged her. She was breathing hard, but she hadn't panicked.

"You wanted to get down a little faster, huh?" I tried to avoid any emotional drama, and she smiled at me.

The next day, she told me she wanted to go back up, and a couple of days later we made a second attempt at the summit. It was terribly cold. A night of gale-force winds forced us to take cover in a cave at 7,200 meters and wait for the sun to come out and make the strongest gusts disappear. When day came, the temperature rose again to normal, but we saw black clouds approaching from the north. When we reached the yellow band,

Emelie decided to go down, and I continued for a few hours. Between the snow and the fog, I couldn't find the summit.

EVERYTHING THAT HAPPENED THAT WEEK REMINDED ME OF THE IMportance of failure, and of failures. We are nothing more than insignificant, fragile people, and this is something we should always keep in mind. Especially when we've grown used to success and we get overconfident. We think we're indestructible and that we can win everything. If we compete, we can be arrogant, but on the mountain, this can end in grief for somebody else.

I guess in one sense, all this made me not want to take any risks—not even one—in this attempt to reach the top of Everest, because right then I didn't feel comfortable climbing this slope on the north face. The challenge of climbing from Rongbuk in one go and without support was already quite big in itself, since I'd never been so far up and didn't know how my body would react.

In today's media, things get trivialized, and we end up thinking that only success has value, whereas failure is a sign of weakness. This leads us to choose between lowering the level of our activities to increase our chances of victory, or accepting failure and criticism, and being patient and stubborn enough to keep trying year after year, until maybe one day we achieve our dream. It's clear that failure doesn't sell. Newspapers, radio, TV, and digital platforms won't talk about mere attempts. People only want to hear about success, because heroes are successful; despite the difficulties, through hard work and persistence, they achieve whatever they set their minds to. No one admires a failure. Sponsors want news from an athlete they can announce with fanfare, and mountain climbers try to reach the highest or most dangerous summit to make the money they need for the next expedition. If a climber doesn't want to take on simpler projects to guarantee a quota of success, the line that separates him from lethal risk gets thinner and thinner. Jean-Christophe Lafaille, Benoît Chamoux, maybe Ueli Steck himself . . . We'll never know why they accepted one risk too many. Media, social, or financial pressure can end up pushing you to say to yourself, *All right, let's do it. You've tried and failed a bunch of times. This time it'll work out.* You put on a blindfold, even just for a moment, and don't see that what you're gambling with is your life. It's really important to detach yourself from this pressure—external or internal—and accept that in mountain climbing, success and failure aren't black-and-white like in other sports. You have to be patient and keep trying year after year, knowing that at least half your attempts won't have the desired result.

I decided to take the normal route along the north-northeastern ridge, and from there, everything sped up. I rested for a day at advanced base camp, at 6,300 meters, and went out for one last acclimation before attacking the summit. After breakfast, I put an ice axe, an anorak, and some thick gloves into my backpack, and set off uphill. First, I reached the North Col without too much effort, then continued along the north ridge, pushing myself along with poles. It was like a Vertical Kilometer, like in Fully, but at a fifth of the speed. It felt perfect. I could keep a consistent, dynamic rhythm, even sprinted to see how my body reacted so I didn't pay for it later. I was considering reaching 8,000 meters and going back down, but I'd come this far in four hours and I was still feeling strong, so I kept going. In less than six hours, I reached the third camp, the last used by commercial expeditions before their final attack on the mountain. I walked through the tents and saw Pemba, the Nepalese guide who was taking clients from the expedition we were sharing a pass with.

"Namasté, Pemba. How's it all going?"

"Great." He took off his oxygen mask. "Where did you come from?" He looked surprised. He hadn't expected to see me there.

"I left the ABC this morning."

"Are you staying to sleep tonight?" I noticed he looked baffled and must've been putting two and two together.

"No, I don't have a tent. And anyway, I sleep better down there. I just came up to take a spin."

"You're a monkey!" He laughed and laughed, staring at me in amazement.

I answered him with a smile, waved goodbye, and kept going slowly until I reached the beginning of the north ridge, at 8,400 meters. I paused when I arrived. The views were lavish, and the sun shone brightly at midafternoon. It was hot, and *Look—I'm up here.* I hesitated a few seconds. I didn't know whether to keep going to the summit; it seemed so close . . . But I decided to stick to the plan: acclimation that day, and wait a week to attack the summit. I stayed there a few minutes to savor the air and the landscape, then started heading down. Since I was feeling good, I started jogging along the snowy slope, and it took me less than three hours to get to the advanced base camp, just in time to clean up a bit, unpack, and have dinner. It was clearly my best day from a physiological standpoint, which showed the success of the acclimation process and confirmed the performance I was capable of at high altitude. If there's one thing I've learned, it's that if I'm feeling good, it's better to keep going up and see what happens, because the altitude doesn't give you too many chances.

IT WAS CURFEW TIME ON MAY 21, AND I FELT LIKE A THIEF STEALING quiet moments out on the mountain, when there shouldn't have been anyone in that area, on a ridge above 8,500 meters, with the sun dipping down behind Cho Oyu. All the mountains around me seemed small, and despite feeling ill—I wanted to throw up and had diarrhea, thanks to gastroenteritis that had shown up at the worst possible moment—I forgot everything and experienced this unique moment intensely, which allowed me to embrace the night in all its serenity and beauty.

For the past four days, I'd been resting at the Rongbuk base camp, and I'd taken the chance to go out running and eat fried potatoes at the Tibetan lodges. Essentially, I'd been getting bored in my tent. Until about twenty hours before, after dinner on May 20, when I'd left the rock-and-powder esplanade at the end of the road that delivered tourists every day, who would take photos of themselves with the highest summit on Earth in the background, and maybe would buy a souvenir where two thousand years ago Milarepa had hidden away in a cave to meditate. I threw my backpack on my back with everything I needed—a down ski suit, some boots with crampons, an ice axe, two poles, a liter of water, fifteen gels and energy bars, a headlamp, gloves, mittens, and sunglasses. I have studied and optimized my equipment selection for years. "Not this. This, no. We can leave this out," is what engineers and designers heard me say whenever I visited them to make prototypes of boots, clothing, or backpacks. I would take an eraser to the paper and start rubbing out the zippers, pockets, and anything that seemed unnecessary, until the design was so simple that it could be drawn with only one line. The boots I was wearing, for example, were like enormous socks lined with insulating material, with carbon fiber soles and crampons already attached. That way, they took up less space and hardly weighed anything. I could set out running in sneakers and, when I reached the snow, pull on those socks with crampons over the top and keep going over the ice.

At ten in the evening I began to run, and spent all night crossing the endless 20-kilometer moraine until I reached the glacier where the advanced base camp was located. I stopped for a couple of hours for a rest and some food and water, waiting for the sun to come out and warm my surroundings before I set off into the snow. With the first rays of light, I pressed forward over the glacier and climbed up as far as the North Col. That was when I began to notice that something wasn't quite right that day. My stomach was unsettled, and every once in a while I retched unexpectedly. By the time I realized it was gastroenteritis, I had already passed 8,000 meters, and the idea of turning back when I was so close to the summit made me feel ashamed. In any case, I was sure I would survive the stomachache and diarrhea. At the most, I was in for a rough time. The diarrhea was the most inconvenient, because it meant I had to unzip my snowsuit and take the top part off so I could take a shit, and up there on the mountain, this was pretty annoying. The solution was not to eat anything. My body could rely on its fat reserves for hours, though it would suffer a drop in energy. But that way I could keep climbing, little by little.

Given that the conditions on the mountain meant there was no chance of an avalanche, now that I was up on a ridge, the only risks, as far as I could tell, were suffering an edema or seizing up from the cold. I kept going slowly, and no worrying symptoms appeared.

When the sun disappeared behind Cho Oyu, I didn't hesitate to keep going. I knew as long as I kept moving constantly I wouldn't have any problems, no matter how cold it got. Step by step, I kept ascending, with no sense of time or worry, embracing the night's gifts of solitude and darkness.

Up there, your sense of time is strange and intuitive. It floats around you, but you can't touch it—it's diffuse. The same happens with your thoughts, which also stand still, and your mind goes blank. It is absorbed in a deep meditation, alien to the body, which fights to move forward at a glacial pace. Only a technical difficulty interrupts this concentration, and for a few seconds your thoughts return to command a precise maneuver, before plunging back into the abyss.

I began to sense that I should have reached the summit a while ago. In the darkness, I couldn't see where the mountain ended, and with every rock that jutted out, I wished I had reached the end of the route, but there was always another. Until the moment came when I glimpsed a ridge in the gloom, felt a breeze, and saw lights slowly twinkling on the other side.

I checked my watch for the first time in many hours and saw it was past midnight. Ahead of me, I saw prayer flags flapping at the mountain's summit. Exhausted and destroyed, I sat down beside the flags and breathed deeply, hanging my head between my knees. Right then, I didn't feel any satisfaction, just a very essential liberation. *Finally, finally I don't have to keep climbing.* To help my recovery along, I took an energy gel from my pocket and ate it. It was the first thing I'd eaten in many hours.

The night was black and bright, and I saw lights like fireflies from the north and south, leaving the last camps to head up to where I was sitting. Satisfaction began to knock at my door. It said, *Yes, I'm in the highest place I can possibly be.* Luckily, exhaustion was more powerful than this feeling and didn't allow my head to lose sight of things and let itself be defeated by the excitement.

Soon, I slowly began to head down. When I reached the pyramid, at 8,700 meters, my stomach urgently demanded that I undo my ski suit and squat. *Damn it, I shouldn't have eaten that gel!* I grabbed a rock and used it, as carefully as was possible under the circumstances, to wipe my ass. It was complicated with mittens so thick. Finally I figured it out and kept going down, laughing to myself about the situation. At the foot of the pyramid, I passed the end of a long, illuminated line of fifty people—porters, guides, and clients—climbing in disciplined silence, tied to the ropes and blocking the way at the most technical stretches. Soon I left the last light in the group behind and I was alone again. I went down along the ridge until the bright sun greeted me. Sheltered from the wind, with the pleasant warmth of the rising sun, I stopped and lay down on the ground. I rested for a while.

More than 8 kilometers away, Emelie didn't know where I was. It had been hours since I should have gotten back to base camp and sent news. The phrase "No news is good news" doesn't apply when the person you love is on a large mountain.

We always think the worst when we don't hear from them. She was imagining me suffering or dead, somewhere up on the highest part. In a hyper-connected world where we find out about everything immediately, I had chosen an experience that was the polar opposite. I wanted to be the only one making decisions up there, with no other influence or external pressure, with no one to encourage me when things were going badly, or to tell me I had to give up because bad weather was coming or I was moving too slowly. That's why I'd left my satellite phone with Séb. That decision, which was making my experience more authentic, was making those who love me suffer. Neither Séb at base camp nor Emelie in Zegama knew where I was or what was happening to me.

Finally, at around midmorning, a good thirty hours after I'd left Rongbuk, I got back to the advanced base camp and met up with Séb. I called home to say all was well and that we'd be leaving soon, but all I could think of was recovering my strength and trying the climb again in a few days' time.

As I was coming down, since I was going slowly, and despite how tired I was, I had time to think. I was a little disappointed with myself. My performance hadn't been as good as five days earlier, and the gastroenteritis had screwed me over. I wanted to do more, and felt like I could. And I began to think it would be good to know if I could climb again after a short time, just like I would in the Alps. When we spent a week in the mountains there, we parked the truck at the bottom of a valley and went out on some expedition every day after breakfast. Could I export that model to the highest peaks of the Himalayas? The only way to find out was to attempt another climb soon. My doubt was whether three days would be long enough for my body to recover from the immense effort it had performed.

THAT SAME DAY, WE TOOK DOWN THE TENTS WE'D PITCHED AT THE advanced base camp and went down to Rongbuk. Conversations at base camp are like those on Wall Street, except that there, instead of speculating about stocks and money, people talk about the weather forecast. One of the few advantages of sharing a space with a commercial expedition from time to time is that they have vast resources and, as a result, have access to the best forecasts. And they agreed that May 27 would be the best day of the season.

Séb and I rested for a couple of days and then it was time to go. We crossed the moraine again to the ABC. Since we didn't have tents there, Monica, the doctor on the expedition with Adrian Ballinger and Cory Richards, who at that moment were climbing Everest without oxygen, invited us to sleep in their tent. I got a few hours' rest, and before the break of dawn I set out again toward the summit.

I walked at a good pace and after a while had already reached the north ridge. Though the forecast had predicted a spectacular day, it had begun with a curtain of high clouds that prevented the sun's heat from getting through, and at 7,000 meters I had to put on my down ski suit to keep warm. Despite my tiredness, I was feeling good and got to 8,300 meters in about seven hours. An hour longer than the acclimation day, but two less than five days ago. I passed a few people on their way down: a Japanese party, who'd done the summit with oxygen, and the German climber Ralf Dujmovits, who'd attempted it without oxygen and was complaining about the cold. I kept going and passed more climbers on their way down.

When I left the ridge, I was greeted by a strong wind, and since it was cold, I put on all the clothes I had. I left my now empty backpack tied to some rocks, and my poles as well, since with the cold and wind I needed to keep my hands low. Before reaching the second step, I ran into Adrian Ballinger, who had achieved his dream of climbing without oxygen. He was with Cory, and some guides and Sherpas. From that moment on, I was alone again on the mountain. The wind didn't let up; on the contrary, gusts were lifting the snow and carrying it to the ridge. At some points I had to open a pretty deep path. My pace was slow, but I was feeling good, and I could handle the cold. My mind was dulled again by the altitude bubble, and I kept going almost robotically, step by step, until dusk. A splendid sunset awaited me at the foot of the pyramid, just 150 meters from the summit.

The wind was making the snow dance against a backdrop of shadows, a gift from the sun as it went down gently behind a sea of high clouds, preventing me from seeing the 8,000-meter peaks around me. The beauty took on a tinge of horror, since it was a prelude to spending another night up there. Every step was a struggle, and my mind wouldn't stop telling me, *Stop. Turn around. There's no need to suffer this much.* And I couldn't find any reason to disagree. But since reason isn't what leads us to climb mountains, I kept going. I counted up to twenty-five steps. I stopped. Twenty-five more. I stopped again to breathe hard, to try to fill my lungs with that thin air.

And that's how I repeated my path from a few days before,

until I saw the snowy ridge appear. *A few meters more and I'll be right next to the flags.* And yes, there they were, this time lashed by a gale-force wind. The only thought that crossed my mind on the summit was to turn around and go down as quickly as possible. Anyway, up there, your emotions only lead you to make the wrong decision. Euphoria distracts you, and fear prevents you from seeing clearly. The wind was assaulting me and the snow was pounding my face. I began to retrace my path.

As I climbed down, the storm swelled and became increasingly violent. Though it wasn't extreme, the snow was intense. The wind stirred everything up, and in the dark of the night, I had to pay close attention not to stray from the path. I felt like I was floating, as if my steps were a long way away. I felt my tiredness and saw my actions as if in a dream. It was as if my body and mind had divorced and each had gone its own way.

I climbed down the Three Steps without any trouble and gradually headed down the mixed slopes to leave the northeast ridge in the direction of the north one. I wasn't aware, but it had been hours since I'd had anything to eat or drink. I'd focused all my energy on the mountain and hadn't thought about anything else.

When I left the rocky channels beneath the ridge, I was having trouble thinking clearly. The simplest calculations required a gargantuan effort. Adding and subtracting had become more challenging than solving a complex equation, and I strained to keep my brain active, since it seemed about to shut down. I knew I'd left my backpack somewhere around there on my way up, but I couldn't find an image of the specific place in my memory. *Where the hell is it? Think, Kilian, think. Let's see if you already passed it. Hey, look, there it is!* I knelt down to pick up my backpack, and that's the last thing I remembered.

BUT WHERE AM I? WHERE THE HELL AM I? SUDDENLY, I REGAINED consciousness. And I saw myself walking along some shelves on a fairly steep wall that I'd never seen before. *How did I get here? Where's the ridge?* Everything around me was black, and the light from my headlamp only showed me the shapes of the rocks in front of me. All I could see was a wall of snow and ice, until darkness swallowed everything up. I had a fleeting memory. *Oof, I know. That's where we crossed last year to leave the wall . . . where the avalanche fell on me! But how the fuck did I get here? What the hell am I doing on the northeast face of the mountain?* I was completely disoriented and couldn't reconstruct the route I had taken to get here after picking up my backpack. I was drawing a blank. I didn't know how long I'd been out of it, or what path I had taken during that parenthesis. *I'll figure it out later. Right now I need to get out of here and find my way.*

When I realized I was on the northeast face, I thought the best thing I could do was to cross toward the left without losing altitude, until I found the ridge again. Then I realized that someone was following about 30 or 40 meters behind me. They were moving slowly and were too far away for me to identify them. The silhouette was clear, and though at that moment I didn't know why, I knew I had to get away from there. In a strange way, I thought that person was responsible for my detour and the fact that I'd ended up there. *Why are they so slow?* They were barely moving, pressing forward only a bit. *Come on, hurry up. I want to get back to the camp!* Although I knew it was a hallucination from the beginning, I had to fight with myself the whole time not to forget that. They followed me as I hewed to the left, increasingly desperate to get onto the ridge, but they didn't appear.

The first spur I came across should have alerted me, since it was much steeper and rockier than I remembered, but I was sure this was a result of the difference between spring and summer. When I reached the second spur, I realized I wasn't where I thought I was. *Right now I should be above the channel I took last year to go up, and I should reach the ridge. This should be the ridge! But why is there nothing here? Where's the goddamned ridge?* The wall of rock went on, getting steeper and steeper, more and more distant in my memory, until I finally I had to admit it. I wasn't on the northeast face. In fact, I had no fucking clue where I was. The person following me disappeared right away. My brain, still tired and cloudy, demanded attention and asked me to think clearly once I'd recognized my disorientation.

I was fine, physically speaking. I didn't fear for my life. I was very tired, yes, extremely tired, but I could feel my body resisting and knew it would still be hard to completely wear it out. It could keep going for as many hours as necessary. The real problem was that I didn't know where I was. I had no idea. I kept going down, trying to find some sign that might give me a clue. I even tried to remember the photos of the mountain I'd studied. It wasn't extreme, but the slope was similar to the south face of Mont Blanc, like the Peuterey Ridge or the Innominata. The terrain was rocky and made up of large sheets of smooth stone, with fairly wide shelves carved into it. Sometimes I was too lazy to climb, so I let myself slide down the sheets, my crampons scraping over the rock until they got stuck. The rock quality was terrible; it wasn't solid. Sometimes it broke when I supported my hands and feet on it, and other times the slope was so steep that I had to take off my mittens and climb down with thin gloves to be able to feel the rock. I kept going down for 100 meters or so, but the slope didn't end, and I didn't recognize anything that could show me the way.

I reached a small rocky channel, a narrow dihedron, and thought maybe I could go down there quickly and jump over some sheets of rock until I reached a small balcony. At my feet, there was only a void. To my left and right, the wall was almost vertical. I sat down, pressing my body as close to the wall as I could to keep away from the drop, sheltering from the snow that fell from the rock embedded in the mountain above me. *Wait, Kilian, before you keep going without knowing where, think a little. If you go down, will you find the glacier where the advanced base camp is located? But if I'm not on the northeast face and I keep going down, what will I find? And what if I have to come back up? Oof.* My thoughts were still too clumsy, heavy, distant, and imprecise. *And what if all this isn't real, if it's a dream, or a nightmare, and I've really been sleeping for hours in the tent back at camp? Maybe . . . I don't remember how I got here and I'm dreaming . . . Well, what a shitty dream! I want to wake up already! I want to be back at camp! Maybe if I jump into the void right now, the fright will wake me, like in the movies. But this isn't a dream . . .* My mind was slow and befuddled. The curtain covering my brain wouldn't let me think clearly. *What do I do? What do I do? Think, think . . . Let's see. I'm tired, I've had hallucinations, I can't think straight. It's the middle of the night and I have no fucking clue where I am. At least I'm feeling okay and I'm strong. Now the priority is not to do anything stupid.*

I decided to stay there, since it was somewhat sheltered, and wait for the sun to come up. In daylight, I'd be able to figure out where I was and decide which way I needed to go. I hugged my knees and closed my eyes to rest, until I fell into a light sleep.

I soon woke up and noticed immediately that my brain had recovered its normal speed and clarity. I thanked it. No, I hadn't been dreaming. I was still on the small platform in the middle of the wall. The first thing I did was look at my watch. *How could I be so stupid not to think of that before?* It was almost two in the morning and I was at an altitude of 8,000 meters. *The GPS! Look at the GPS!* Suddenly I remembered I had activated my GPS, and I checked the navigation curve on my watch. I saw a line that went down straight and then suddenly veered to the left at a ninety-degree angle, and continued in that direction for what must have been the equivalent of a kilometer. *Of course, I'm on the north face!* My brain kicked into gear, gathered the information stored in my memory, reviewed the photos of the mountain I'd been scanning mentally for months. *I must be on the stone walls around the Norton Couloir. If I can figure out a way to get down to 7,600, that's where the snow crossing that Messner followed is, and I'll be able to get back to the ridge without any trouble.*

I was greeted by a feeling of relief. Finally, I had no doubt where I was. The situation was still precarious, because I was in a steep and not very stable spot with brittle rock, and it was still a long way back to the ridge. When we climb a mountain, we entrust our body to it, until we reach the bottom and it becomes ours again. I climbed a few meters to make it back over the embedded rock until I found some ground where I was more comfortable and began to cross it, heading down toward the right. The sheets of rock, a few spurs, snow channels, and strips of stone guided me in the darkness until I reached the north ridge again.

At least I was in control of my own movements. During the night, it had been as if someone inside me had taken over and made the general decisions without consulting me, ignoring me as if I were a nobody. And for some unknown reason, that person had decided they wanted to go to the north face. Well, congratulations.

WITH DAYLIGHT CAME THE COMFORT OF THE NORTH RIDGE, BLAN-keted in almost a meter of recently fallen snow. Savoring the feeling of being back up there in summer, with all the fresh snow, and no one else on the mountain, I slid down on my ass until I heard the murmur of voices at the camp. As I slid down the last snowy slopes, I saw someone approaching the foot of the glacier. It was Séb. He offered me a drink of water, and I took a sip that brought me back to life.

When we got to the camp, I ate a little, though my stomach was still shut off, and without wasting any time, we said good-bye to Adrian, Cory, and Monica, grateful that they had let me sleep in their tent. We jogged the 20 kilometers of the moraine back to Rongbuk for the last time, arriving just in time to pack up. The next morning a car would be waiting to take us to Lhasa to catch a plane. We were going home.

Epilogue:
The Welcome

The ferry closed its doors and began to plough through the water. I bought a waffle in the cafeteria and went out on deck. The fresh air and humidity contrasted with the dry atmosphere of the Himalayas. I ran my index finger over my sunburned lips and looked at my almost black hands, wrinkled from dryness. But when I looked up, I forgot the high mountains. The breeze and the smell of the sea brought me back to the Norwegian fjords.

The boat was quickly approaching land, but the half-hour journey seemed to go on forever. Before we docked, I had already slung my backpack over my shoulder, and when the ramp began to lower, I saw Emelie waiting for me, with the car engine on. We kissed in silence and then set off. We said everything without opening our mouths to speak.

I left my backpack in the house and took off the sweaty clothes I'd worn for the two-day journey from the dusty camp, and then we put on our sneakers and went out for a run. We ran side by side without speaking for a good while, savoring the sound of the wind and the synchronized rhythm of our breath. As the kilometers went by, our words began to seek a path and find their way. And little by little, the conversation left memories behind and settled back into the day-to-day. It was as if we'd returned to that morning I went out to run up one of the surrounding peaks.

"This Saturday there's a race in Geiranger and I was thinking of going. You want to come?" Emelie.

"Yeah, it could be good to get back into the competition rhythm." Me.

We ran for a couple of hours through the fog, the wet grass, and the snow still covering the peaks. When we got home, I found my luggage still waiting to be unpacked. I began to empty it out into two separate piles: dirty clothes and equipment to put away. I soon left it half done, picked up the clothes I'd taken out and put them into the washing machine. There were still some things left to take out of my backpack. I always leave some reserves in there so I'm ready to take off again.

Summer was knocking at the door; the snow on the peaks was disappearing swiftly, and the flowers were taking their turn to begin to bloom. In a just a few weeks the landscape would change so much that no one would remember that those meadows of such intense and varied colors, and so bursting with life, had been shrouded in white.

In my mind, my memories of Everest were also melting quickly, like snow that vanishes from the surface and infuses the earth with fresh life in its new state. And this forgetting made my learning flourish, and my excitement began to stir again. I was already looking forward to the race the following weekend, to new expeditions, to new ideas that would make new attempts possible . . .

Some of my friends, who know me well, are surprised when they come to visit, not to see trophies on display on the shelves, full of books and maps. But I'm afraid to end up as a prisoner of my past. Maybe that's why I've never kept any trophy from the races I've won. Sometimes my grandfather wants them, sometimes I give them to a kid beaming with excitement who's followed a race. Or to the owner of a hotel we stayed in, or to a sponsor. Some end up disassembled in a recycling bin, or sometimes I've used them to scrape the wax off my skis, or as a vegetable chopping board. Is it fear of being stuck in the past that drives me, or vanity? Maybe what makes me feel so vain is just my discomfort with accepting recognition.

"One day you'll regret not having enjoyed everything you're achieving." Emelie acts like she's telling me off.

One thing I know is that I've had a great time, an excellent time, both in planning and undertaking the expedition. But success has shown me that in the end it wasn't so hard. And the only point of it is to make me think about how to go further.

THE NIGHT WAS SHORT, AND I WENT OUT EARLY TO RUN IN THE MOUN-tains again. Right by our house, I took a narrow, steep path among wet rocks and fallen branches, that led me away from the fjords and into the mountains, to the ground where tall grasses and insects don't bother you, where only the rocks and a few plants dare to live. A fine rain hung in the sky, and the ridge I wanted to climb was playing hide-and-seek with the fog.

It was an easy ridge. According to the book of reviews I had at home, it was a Norwegian grade IV, which meant it was terrain I could normally move over with ease and skill. It was one of the few simple ridges near home that I still hadn't done, and since I had to relax a little before the next race, I made the most of that stupid day by exploring it. My feet slipped on wet rocks, but I kept going since I could hold on well with my hands. The ridge narrowed until it became a sharp blade like a knife, and the stone, not terribly stable, didn't seem like it wanted to be my friend. I continued along the edge. The wind and rain buffeted me back and forth, and after a while I asked myself what the hell I was doing up there. I had just gotten back from Everest, but a mountain just over 1,000 meters was reminding me that every mountain, large or small, decides whether or not to offer us the dance we want.

THAT SATURDAY, I PINNED A NUMBER ON MYSELF AGAIN AND RAN MY first paved half marathon. It was an uphill race along a road.

On our way home in the car, Emelie took out a piece of paper and started writing down all the races we wanted to run that summer. Since we realized we had a free weekend, we considered the peaks we wanted to climb and the journeys we'd like to take. When we went to bed, there was no blank space left on the paper on either side—the margins were full of tiny handwritten notes, with names of peaks, routes, and races, and so many ideas that maybe we'd never have time for them all.

We agreed that it was possible that one summer or year, or maybe our entire lives, wouldn't be long enough. But we decided it was worth giving it a try.

Unless an avalanche, a rock, or old age comes for me first, I'll keep climbing mountains, in love with that naked feeling of lightness. I'll keep on moving until my body's resources are spent and it can't keep up with my mind anymore. I'm convinced that the best time is always now, and the best memory is always tomorrow.

A SUNBEAM CAME INTO THE BEDROOM, NOT KNOCKING TO ASK PERmission, and a gentle gust of wind moved the curtains. I turned over to try to keep sleeping, but it was already too late. I stretched out my arm and, disappointed, found only a wrinkled sheet. I lazed in bed for a while, shaking off sleep by gradually stretching.

On the nightstand, the clock said six in the morning, and through the window I glimpsed a bright, blue sky. The wind tried to stir the curtains again and filtered in, bringing a gust of fresh air and the scent of spring forests. When I got up, I felt my joints creak a little and noticed my legs felt dry and heavy.

The sun took over the room completely, and outside the grass, moistened by the overnight frost, gave off a youthful breath. The shirt and pants I'd worn for yesterday's race still lay on a chair by the window. I gave them a sniff and decided I hadn't sweated too much. I put on the pants, and as I pulled the T-shirt over my head, I heard the door open and a sprightly voice say:

"What's up? Shall we go for a run?"

About the Author

Kilian Jornet is the best mountain athlete in the world. For the past fifteen years he has dominated the ski-mountaineering and trail-running scene, winning all major championships and races.

He grew up in a mountain hut in the Spanish Pyrenees, and the mountains have always been his playground—whether he is running, climbing, or skiing. As a multidisciplinary athlete, he also holds speed records in mountains around the world, including a double ascent to Mount Everest.

Nowadays, Kilian lives in Norway, where he keeps exploring his limits in mountain sports and inspiring a large community with movies, books, and digital content.

Kilian has also become a climate advocate who is working to raise awareness about the need to protect our environment.

ALSO BY KILIAN JORNET

Run or Die
Summits of My Life